INTERMITTENT FASTING FOR WOMEN OVER 60

The complete guide to unlock your metabolism and lose weight

Verna.I.Mary

1

Table of Contents

Introduction

Helen was a woman in her mid-sixties. She had been overweight for most of her life and had tried many different diets over the years, but nothing seemed to work. She was feeling discouraged and frustrated, until one day she stumbled upon this book called "Intermittent Fasting for Women over 60" while browsing in her local bookstore.

The book outlined the benefits of intermittent fasting and how it could help her lose weight and improve her overall health. Helen was intrigued and decided to give it a try. She began fasting for 16 hours each day, eating only during the remaining 8 hours.

At first, she found it difficult to stick to her new eating schedule. But after a few weeks, her cravings lessened and she started to lose weight. She quickly began to feel more energized and healthier. After a few months, she had lost a significant amount of weight, and her friends and family were amazed by the transformation.

Helen was so pleased with her progress that she began to incorporate other healthful habits into her routine, such as exercising regularly and eating more nutritious foods. She even took up yoga and meditation.

Helen's story is a testament to the power of intermittent fasting and the positive changes it can bring about. She was able to take control of her health and her life, and she achieved her goals with the help of this simple book.

If you've been considering trying intermittent fasting, you've come to the right place. This book is your definitive guide to learning what intermittent fasting is, how to do it effectively and safely, and how to make it part of your lifestyle.

Intermittent fasting is a powerful approach to health, nutrition, and weight loss that allows you to improve your overall wellness and reduce your risk of developing certain diseases. It is a form of dieting that cycles between periods of fasting and eating, and it can be tailored to fit your individual lifestyle and goals.

This book will provide you with the knowledge you need to make an informed decision about whether or not intermittent fasting is right for you. You'll learn the basics of intermittent fasting, its potential benefits, and the different types of fasting that are available. You'll also get an in-depth look at how to plan and adjust your meals for maximum results, as well as how to stay mindful and motivated throughout your fasting journey.

By the end of this book, you'll be well-equipped to make the most of this powerful dietary practice and reap the rewards that come with it. So, if you're ready to take control of your health and well-being, let's get started!

Part One: Intermittent Fasting Basics

Intermittent fasting is a type of dieting pattern in which you cycle between periods of eating and fasting. It does not dictate which foods you should eat, but rather when you should eat them. It has become a popular weight loss strategy and is often used in conjunction with a low-calorie diet to achieve desired results.

The most common type of intermittent fasting is the 16/8 method, where you fast for 16 hours per day and eat within an 8-hour window. This means that you are essentially skipping breakfast and having a late lunch, followed by an early dinner. Other popular intermittent fasting methods include the 5:2 diet, which involves eating normally 5 days of the week, and fasting for two days, and alternate-day fasting, where you fast every other day.

When following an intermittent fasting plan, you should focus on eating whole, unprocessed foods that are high in fiber, lean protein, and healthy fats. This will ensure that you are getting all the essential nutrients your body needs, while still staying within your calorie goals. Additionally, it is important to stay hydrated by drinking plenty of water throughout the day.

Intermittent fasting can be an effective way to lose weight, as it helps to reduce calorie intake and encourage fat burning. However, it is important to remember that it is not a quick fix and should be done in combination with a healthy diet and regular exercise. Additionally, if you have any medical conditions or take any medication, it is important to speak to your doctor before beginning any type of diet or fasting program.

Overall, intermittent fasting is a safe and effective tool for weight loss when done in combination with a healthy diet and regular physical activity. It can help to reduce calorie intake and encourage fat burning, while still providing your body with the essential nutrients it needs. If you are considering intermittent fasting, it is important to speak to your doctor first and make sure that it is the right approach for you.

Chapter 1: What is Intermittent Fasting?

Intermittent fasting is a dietary pattern that allows you to switch between periods of eating and fasting. It involves reducing calorie intake for a certain period of time, usually between 16–24 hours. During this period of fasting, no food or drinks that contain calories are consumed. Intermittent fasting is thought to have many health benefits, including weight loss, improved digestion, and a decreased risk of certain chronic diseases. It is also thought to help improve mental clarity and focus. In addition, it may help reduce inflammation, lower cholesterol, and improve cardiovascular health. Intermittent fasting can be done in several different ways, such as skipping breakfast, eating all meals within a certain window of time, or limiting calorie intake to specific days of the week. It is important to speak with a healthcare provider before beginning any fasting regimen, as it may not be suitable for everyone.

Intermittent fasting is a popular trend among health and fitness enthusiasts. It is thought to lead to weight loss and improved overall health.

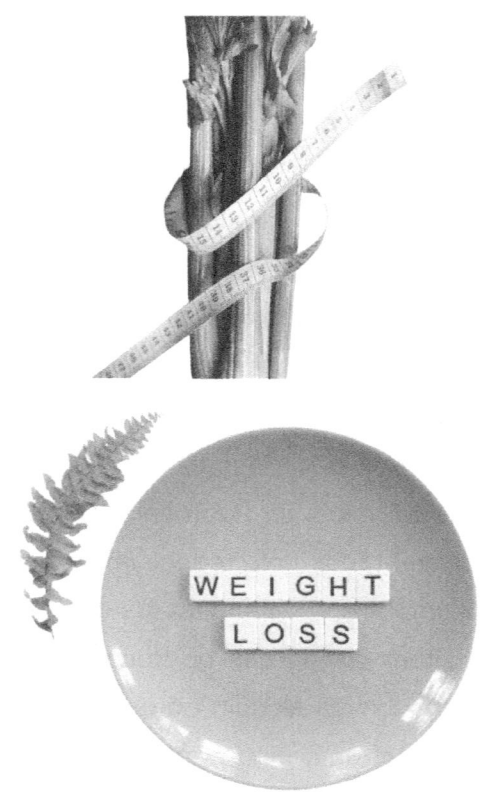

Chapter 2: Benefits of Intermittent Fasting

Intermittent fasting can be an effective way for women over 60 to improve their overall health and well-being. Here are some of the potential benefits:

1) Weight Loss: Intermittent fasting can help to reduce overall calorie intake, which can lead to weight loss. This can help to reduce the risk of obesity-related diseases, such as diabetes and heart disease.

2) Improved Metabolism: Intermittent fasting can help to increase metabolic rate, which can help to promote more efficient calorie burning and weight loss.

3) Improved Cognitive Function: Intermittent fasting can improve cognitive function, making it easier to focus and remember things.

4) Improved Hormonal Balance: Intermittent fasting can help to regulate hormones, which can reduce the risk of hormone-related diseases, such as breast cancer.

5) Reduced Inflammation: Intermittent fasting can help to reduce inflammation, which can reduce the risk of chronic diseases, such as arthritis and Alzheimer's disease.

6) Improved Energy Levels: Intermittent fasting can help to increase energy levels, making it easier to stay physically active and maintain a healthy lifestyle.

7) Improved Immune System: Intermittent fasting can help to boost the immune system, reducing the risk of infection and illness.

8) Lower Blood Pressure: Intermittent fasting can help to reduce blood pressure, reducing the risk of hypertension and stroke.

Chapter 3: Types of Intermittent Fasting

1. The 16/8 Method: This involves fasting for 16 hours each day and eating all your meals within an 8-hour window.

The 16/8 Method of intermittent fasting is an increasingly popular method of fasting, especially among women over 60. This method involves fasting for 16 hours a day and eating only during an 8-hour "feeding window". This period of fasting is sometimes referred to as "time-restricted eating". The 16/8 Method of intermittent fasting is believed to offer several health benefits and has become increasingly popular with older women, who may be looking for ways to improve their health and well-being.

The 16/8 Method of intermittent fasting involves splitting the day into two parts, with 16 hours of fasting and 8 hours of eating. During the 16-hour fasting period, no food or calorie-containing drinks should be consumed. During the 8-hour eating window, women over 60 should aim to eat healthy, nutrient-dense meals that are low in sugar and processed foods. Women should also be mindful of their portion sizes and strive to eat until they are satisfied but not overly full.

The 16/8 Method of intermittent fasting has been found to offer numerous health benefits for women over 60. Studies have found that it can help reduce inflammation, improve cardiovascular health, and support weight loss. Additionally, intermittent fasting has been found to help improve metabolic health, reduce oxidative stress, and improve blood sugar levels.

The 16/8 Method of intermittent fasting is a safe and effective way for women over 60 to gain many of the health benefits associated with fasting. However, it's important to note that fasting is not suitable for everyone and should be discussed with a healthcare provider before beginning. Additionally, women should ensure that their fasting and eating windows are tailored to their individual needs and preferences.

2. The 5:2 Diet: This type of intermittent fasting involves eating normally for five days out of the week and then restricting your calorie intake to 500–600 calories on two days of the week.

The 5:2 Diet of intermittent fasting for women over 60 is a diet plan that involves eating fewer calories on two days of the week and eating normally the other five days. This type of fasting helps to reduce calorie intake without eliminating food altogether, making it an ideal diet for many women over 60.

On the two fasting days, women should limit their calorie intake to 500-600 calories, depending on their individual needs. This can be achieved through a combination of low-calorie foods, such as vegetables, fruits, lean proteins, and whole grains. Your meal plan should contain nutrient-dense foods that are low in calories and high in fiber.

The other five days of the week, women should eat a healthy, balanced diet that is low in saturated fat, cholesterol, and added sugars. You should choose from a variety of fruits and vegetables, whole grains, lean proteins, and healthy fats while you stay hydrated by drinking plenty of water.

In addition to a healthy diet, exercise is an important part of the 5:2 Diet for women over 60. The American Heart Association recommends at least 150 minutes of moderate-intensity physical activity or 75 minutes of vigorous-intensity physical activity per week. This can include walking, swimming, cycling, or other activities that you enjoy. The 5:2 Diet of intermittent fasting for women over 60 can be an effective way to reduce calorie intake and lose weight. It can also help to improve overall health by providing the body with essential nutrients and aiding in the prevention of chronic diseases.

3. Eat-Stop-Eat: This type of intermittent fasting involves fasting for 24 hours once or twice a week.

The Eat-Stop-Eat Method of intermittent fasting is a popular dieting strategy that can be beneficial for women over 60. This method involves fasting for 24 hours, followed by a 24 hour period of eating normally. During the fasting period, no food or calorie-containing drinks are allowed.

The Eat-Stop-Eat Method of intermittent fasting has many potential benefits for women over 60. It can help to reduce inflammation, regulate hormones, and promote weight loss. It also reduce the chances of you getting chronic diseases such as diabetes, heart disease, and cancer. Additionally, this method of intermittent fasting can improve mental clarity, increase energy levels, and even help to slow down the ageing process.

However, this method of intermittent fasting is not suitable for everyone. It is important to consult a doctor before starting this type of fasting. Women over 60 may need to adjust the fasting period to ensure they are consuming enough nutrients and staying healthy.

To begin the Eat-Stop-Eat Method of intermittent fasting, women over 60 should start with a 24-hour fast. During this time, no food or calorie-containing beverages should be consumed. Women over 60 should also drink plenty of water during the fasting period to ensure that they stay hydrated.

4. The Warrior Diet: This type of intermittent fasting involves eating one large meal at night and fasting for the rest of the day.

The Warrior Diet Method of intermittent fasting for women over 60 is a way of eating that focuses on eating one large meal in the evening, and fasting during the daytime hours. This approach to nutrition provides many benefits for older women, including weight loss, improved mental clarity and focus, and a reduction in inflammation.

During the day, women on the Warrior Diet consume only small snacks consisting of fresh fruits, vegetables, and nuts. This helps to reduce cravings and provide important nutrients. Additionally, by eating fewer meals throughout the day, older women benefit from increased energy levels and improved digestion.

In the evening, the Warrior Diet encourages women to consume a single meal that is high in protein and healthy fats, such as fish, eggs, or a lean cut of meat. This meal should also include complex carbohydrates, such as sweet potatoes, quinoa, and brown rice. Eating a larger meal helps to provide a feeling of satiety and can help to reduce cravings.

In addition to the dietary changes, the Warrior Diet also encourages older women to engage in regular exercise. This can include light aerobic activity, such as walking or swimming, and strength training. Regular exercise helps to improve muscle tone, reduce risk of injury, and improve overall well being. Finally, the Warrior Diet encourages women over 60 to practice mindful eating. This involves slowing down their eating and paying attention to how their body responds to the food they are consuming. Mindful eating helps to reduce overeating and promote a healthier relationship with food.

The Warrior Diet is an effective method of intermittent fasting for women over 60 that is safe, easy to follow, and provides numerous health benefits. By following this approach to nutrition, older women can experience improved overall health and wellbeing.

5. Alternate-Day Fasting: This type of intermittent fasting involves alternating between days of eating normally and days of fasting.

ADF is becoming increasingly popular among women over 60, as it is believed to have a variety of health benefits.

The most common form of ADF involves consuming no food or very few calories on the fasting days, and then "feasting" on regular meals on the non-fasting days. This approach allows the body to take a break from digesting and storing calories, and is thought to have a variety of health benefits.

The most researched benefit of ADF is its ability to help with weight loss. Studies have shown that ADF can induce significant weight loss in overweight and obese women over 60. This is thought to be due to the lowered calorie consumption associated with the fasting days, as well as the body's increased sensitivity to insulin, which helps regulate body weight.

ADF is also believed to help reduce inflammation and improve overall health. Studies have shown that ADF may reduce levels of inflammatory markers in the body, which can help reduce the risk of chronic diseases such as diabetes and heart disease. Furthermore, ADF may also improve cognitive function, as it is thought to increase the production of brain-derived neurotrophic factor (BDNF), a protein involved in the formation of new neural connections in the brain.

For women over 60, ADF may be an effective way to improve health and lose weight. This type of fasting should always be done under the supervision of a healthcare professional, as there are risks associated with fasting for extended periods of time.

Part Two: Intermittent Fasting for Women Over 60

Intermittent fasting has become increasingly popular among people of all ages and genders. However, it can be especially beneficial for women over 60. Intermittent fasting is a dietary pattern that involves switching between periods of eating and fasting. During the fasting periods, you consume either no calories or very few calories. There are several types of intermittent fasting, including the 16/8 method, the 5:2 diet, and alternate-day fasting. The health benefits of intermittent fasting for women over 60 are numerous. It may help reduce inflammation, improve mental clarity, increase energy levels, and promote weight loss.

Intermittent fasting may be beneficial for reducing symptoms of many age-related diseases, including heart disease, diabetes, and certain types of cancer.

Intermittent fasting is a safe and healthy way to lose weight for women over 60. By restricting the number of calories consumed each day, you can achieve a calorie deficit and promote weight loss. Additionally, intermittent fasting can help reduce muscle loss, which is a common side effect of aging.

Intermittent fasting also improves cognitive function with women. Studies have shown that fasting can improve memory and reduce the risk of developing Alzheimer's disease. Additionally, intermittent fasting may be beneficial for reducing stress and improving mood.

Finally, intermittent fasting can help improve heart health. Studies have found that fasting can reduce cholesterol levels and decrease the risk of developing heart disease.

Intermittent fasting is a safe and healthy way to improve overall health for women over 60. Before starting any type of diet, it's important to consult with your doctor to ensure it's the right choice for you.

Additionally, it's important to ensure that you're getting all the necessary nutrients during your non-fasting periods.

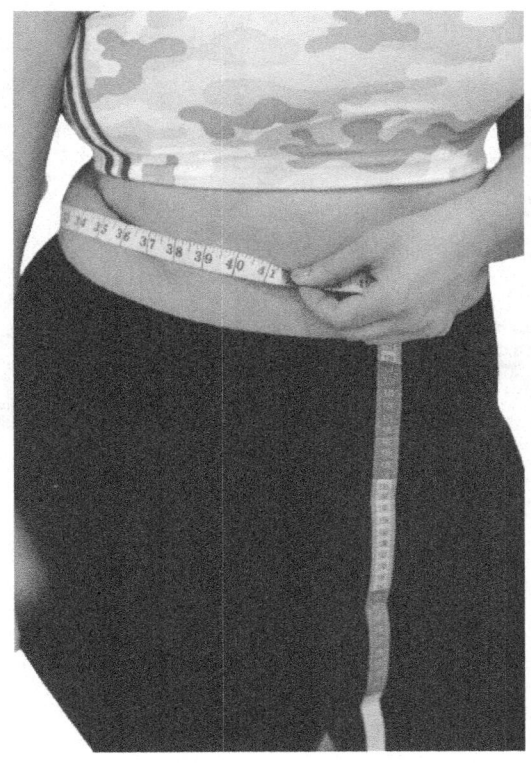

Chapter 4: Understanding the Unique Needs of Women Over 60

Women over 60 represent an often overlooked demographic when it comes to healthcare, lifestyle, and mental health. Because of their age, women over 60 may face unique challenges that require extra attention from healthcare providers, family, and friends. Understanding the unique needs of this population can help ensure women over 60 receive the care and support they need to remain healthy and happy.

First and foremost, women over 60 are more likely to experience chronic illnesses and conditions such as cancer, heart disease, diabetes, and arthritis. Regular health check-ups, screenings, and physical activity can help to reduce the risk of such illnesses and conditions. Additionally, women over 60 may need assistance with managing their medications and understanding the side effects of those medications.

Women over 60 may also be more likely to experience loneliness, isolation, and depression due to the loss of loved ones and the reduction in social activities. Encouraging socialization and providing companionship can help to reduce the risk of depression in this population. Additionally, providing resources to support mental health, such as counseling and support groups, can be beneficial.

Women over 60 also need to be mindful of their nutrition. As people age, their nutritional needs may change, and they may need to make changes in their diets to ensure they receive the nutrients they need. Additionally, regular physical activity is important for maintaining good health. Women over 60 may need assistance in finding activities that are enjoyable and safe for their age group.

Finally, women over 60 may need assistance in navigating the healthcare system. This can include understanding insurance coverage, determining what services are covered, and understanding the costs associated with healthcare. Additionally, it is important to make sure women over 60 have someone to help them advocate for their healthcare needs.

Understanding the unique needs of women over 60 is essential for providing the best care and support possible. Knowing the risks associated with aging, providing resources for mental health and socialization, addressing nutrition and physical activity needs, and ensuring access to the healthcare system can help ensure women over 60 maintain the highest quality of life possible.

Chapter 5: Intermittent Fasting Guidelines for Women Over 60

The following are the intermittent fasting guidelines for women over 60:

A) Aim to fast for 12-14 hours per day- This can be done by skipping breakfast and having an early dinner so that you are not eating for at least 12 hours. Fasting for 12-14 hours per day is a great way to give your body the time it needs to rest, repair, and cleanse itself. This type of fasting can help improve your overall health and well-being, and can also be used as a weight-loss tool. Here are some tips on how to aim to fast for 12-14 hours per day.

1. Choose your fasting window: Before you begin fasting, decide on the time frame that works best for you. Many people find that 12-14 hours of fasting from dinner to breakfast, or from breakfast to dinner, is the most manageable.

2. Prepare for fasting: Don't try to jump into a 12-14 hour fast without any preparation. Take the time to plan out your meals and snacks for the day before you start your fast. This will help you stick to your fasting window and prevent overeating.

3. Eat nutrient-dense meals: During your eating window, focus on consuming nutrient-dense meals and snacks that are high in fiber, protein, and healthy fats. These types of foods will help keep you full and energized throughout your fasting window.

4. Stay hydrated: Drinking plenty of water is essential during fasting. It's important to stay hydrated to prevent dehydration and to flush out toxins from your body.

5. Get enough rest: Getting enough rest and sleep is important for your overall health and well-being, and especially so when fasting. Make sure you get 7-8 hours of sleep a night to ensure your body has the time to rest and repair.

6. Don't overdo it: Fasting for 12-14 hours per day can be a powerful tool for improving your health, but it's important to remember that it's not a one-size-fits-all approach. It should be carried out

as fun and not an activity to push your body too hard. If you're feeling tired or weak, take a break and adjust your fasting window accordingly.

Fasting for 12-14 hours per day can be a great way to give your body the rest and nourishment it needs. Just remember to be mindful of your body and adjust your fasting window accordingly. With these tips, you can easily aim to fast for 12-14 hours per day and reap the benefits that come along with it.

B) Increase your fasting time gradually if you are able to tolerate it-

If you're a woman over 60 looking to increase your fasting time, it can be done gradually. Start by fasting for 12-16 hours, then gradually increase the time each day until you can fast for 20-24 hours. Drink enough water to stay hydrated throughout the day. You can also snack on healthy foods such as fruits, vegetables, nuts and seeds. This will help keep your energy levels up and make it easier to tolerate the fasting period. Additionally, it's important to listen to your body and make sure you don't push yourself too hard. If you start to feel weak or dizzy, take a break and eat something. With practice and patience, you should be able to comfortably increase your fasting time.

C) Limit your calorie intake throughout the day to ensure that you are not overeating or indulging in unhealthy snacks-

If you want to limit your calorie intake throughout the day, it is important to plan ahead and be mindful of what you are eating. Start your day with a healthy breakfast that is full of protein, complex carbohydrates, and healthy fats. This will provide you with energy and keep you full for longer. Avoid sugary snacks and drinks and opt for healthier options such as fruits, nuts, and yogurt.

When it comes to lunch and dinner, focus on lean proteins and complex carbohydrates such as quinoa, brown rice, and beans. Include plenty of fresh vegetables and fruits, and try to limit your intake of processed foods. If you are feeling hungry in between meals, reach for a healthy snack such as a piece of fruit or a handful of nuts.

Finally, be aware of your portion sizes. Make sure you are eating the right amount of food and not overeating. It is also important to stay hydrated throughout the day, as this can help you feel fuller and more satiated. By planning ahead and being mindful of your food choices, you can limit your calorie intake and ensure that you are not overeating.

D) Stay hydrated with enough water for the day-

Staying hydrated is especially important for women over 60, as dehydration can cause a variety of health issues. Adequate water intake helps support healthy kidney function, which is key to keeping the body's electrolyte balance in check. Additionally, the body's cells need water to function properly, and water is needed to help the body absorb nutrients. Staying hydrated can also help reduce fatigue, headaches, and feelings of confusion or disorientation. Finally, adequate water intake helps keep skin looking healthy and may reduce the risk of developing bladder infections.

E) Nutrient-dense foods-Eat nutrient-dense foods and focus on healthy sources of protein, such as

lean meats, eggs, and legumes. Women over 60 have unique dietary needs. Eating nutrient-dense foods is one of the best ways to ensure that these needs are met. Nutrient-dense foods are those that provide a significant amount of vitamins, minerals, and other essential nutrients, with relatively few calories. Some examples of nutrient-dense foods for women over 60 include whole grains, legumes, nuts and seeds, fruits and vegetables, lean meats and fish, low-fat dairy, and healthy oils. Eating a variety of nutrient-dense foods can help women over 60 maintain good health, reduce the risk of chronic diseases, and promote healthy aging.

F) Avoid sugary or processed foods- Eating a healthy diet is especially important for women over 60. To maintain good health, avoid sugary and processed foods as much as possible. These foods can contain large amounts of added sugars and unhealthy fats, which can lead to weight gain, increase the risk of health problems, and reduce life expectancy. Instead, choose whole foods that are lower in added sugars and unhealthy fats, such as fruits, vegetables, whole grains, lean proteins, and healthy fats. Eating a healthy diet can help to maintain a healthy weight, reduce the risk of chronic diseases, and boost overall health.

G) Exercise- Exercise regularly, as this can help to improve your overall health and wellbeing. Exercising regularly is important for all women, especially those over 60. Regular physical activity can improve overall health, reduce the risk of chronic diseases, and help promote healthy aging. Exercise can also help increase energy levels, reduce stress, and improve mood. Some of the benefits of exercise for women over 60 include improved strength and balance, increased flexibility, better sleep, and improved cognitive function. Regular exercise can also help reduce the risk of falls and fractures, and improve bone health. Exercising regularly is the key to maintaining a healthy lifestyle and achieving optimal health for women over 60.

H) Talk to your doctor before beginning any type of intermittent fasting program-

Talking to your doctor before beginning any type of intermittent fasting program is essential for ensuring the safety and health of your body. Intermittent fasting can be a great way to lose weight, improve energy levels and even boost your immune system. However, it's important to discuss this with your doctor to make sure that it's the right type of fasting for you, and that you're healthy enough to do so. Your doctor can also recommend the best type of intermittent fasting program for you, as well as provide advice on how to stay healthy while you're fasting. Additionally, they can monitor your progress and make sure that you're not doing anything that could potentially harm your health. Ultimately, talking to your doctor before beginning any type of intermittent fasting program is essential for safeguarding your health.

Chapter 6: How to Get Started with Intermittent Fasting

Intermittent fasting is an increasingly popular dietary approach that can be used to improve health and longevity when done correctly. It has been used for centuries in many cultures around the world, but has recently gained popularity in the Western world due to its potential health benefits. Women over 60 can benefit from intermittent fasting, as it can help to reduce inflammation and reduce the risk of age-related diseases. Here is a guide on how to get started with intermittent fasting as a beginner for women over 60:

1. Understand the Basics: Intermittent fasting involves alternating periods of eating and fasting. There are a few different methods of intermittent fasting, including time-restricted feeding, the 5:2 diet, and alternate-day fasting. Generally, these methods involve limiting your eating window to 8-12

hours and fasting for the remaining hours of the day.

2. Consult Your Doctor: Before you start any diet plan, it is important to consult with a doctor or registered dietitian. Your doctor can assess your overall health and determine if intermittent fasting is right for you. They can also help you create a plan that works for your individual needs and goals.

3. Start Small: Start by gradually reducing your eating window to 8-12 hours. You can begin by skipping breakfast and eating from noon to 8 pm, for example. As you become more comfortable with the idea of fasting, you can gradually reduce your eating window further.

4. Hydrate: Make sure to drink plenty of water throughout the day to stay hydrated. Drinking herbal teas can also help to reduce hunger and cravings.

5. Eat Healthy: Eating a balanced diet is key to any successful diet plan. Make sure to include plenty of fresh fruits and vegetables, lean proteins, and healthy fats in your diet.

6. Avoid Sugary Foods: Sugary foods can increase hunger and cravings and can sabotage your efforts.

Avoid processed foods, sugary drinks, and sweets while you are fasting.

7. Exercise: Exercise can help to increase your metabolism, improve your overall health, and reduce stress. Try to incorporate some form of exercise into your routine, such as walking, yoga, or light weight training.

8. Get Support: Starting any new diet plan can be difficult, so it is important to have support from family and friends. Having a supportive environment can help you stay motivated and on track.

Intermittent fasting can be a great tool for women over 60 to improve health and longevity. Make sure to consult with your doctor before starting any new diet plan, and remember to start small, hydrate, eat healthy, and get support. With a few simple tips and the right approach, you can get started with intermittent fasting and start to reap the health benefits.

Chapter 7: 30 days meal plan for Intermittent Fasting

Day 1: **Breakfast**: Smoothie made with banana, 1/2 scoop of protein powder, almond milk, and 1/2 cup of oats. Preparation Method:

1. In a blender, combine 1 banana, 1/2 scoop of protein powder, 1/2 cup of oats and 1 cup of almond milk.

2. Blend until smooth.

3. Pour the smoothie into a glass and enjoy!

Prep Time: 5 minutes

Lunch: Chicken salad with feta cheese, tomatoes, and cucumbers.

Prep Time: 15 minutes

Ingredients:

- 2 chicken breasts

- 1/2 cup feta cheese crumbled

- 2 tomatoes diced

- 1 cucumber diced

- 1/4 cup mayonnaise

- 2 tablespoons red wine vinegar

- 2 tablespoons olive oil

- 1 teaspoon garlic powder

- Salt and pepper to taste

Method:

1. Heat a large skillet over medium-high heat.

2. Rub chicken breasts with 1 tablespoon of olive oil and season with garlic powder, salt, and pepper.

3. Place chicken breasts in skillet and cook for 5-7 minutes per side, until cooked through.

4. Remove chicken from skillet and let cool.

5. Once cooled, dice chicken into small cubes.

6. In a large bowl, combine diced chicken, feta cheese, tomatoes, and cucumber.

7. In a separate bowl, whisk together mayonnaise, red wine vinegar, and remaining tablespoon of olive oil.

8. Pour dressing over chicken mixture and gently toss to combine.

9. Serve immediately, or chill in refrigerator for up to 4 hours.

Snack: A handful of almonds.

Dinner: Baked fish with a side of roasted veggies.

Preparation Method:

1. Preheat oven to 400°F.

2. Line a baking sheet with foil and lightly grease with cooking oil.

3. Place the fish fillets on the baking sheet and season with salt and pepper to taste.

4. In a separate bowl, combine the vegetables with olive oil, salt, and pepper.

5. Place the vegetables around the fish on the baking sheet and bake for 20-25 minutes, or until the fish is cooked through and the vegetables are tender.

6. Serve warm with a lemon wedge.

Prep Time: 10 minutes

Cook Time: 25 minutes

Day 2: **Breakfast**: Oatmeal with blueberries and almond milk.

Preparation Method:

1. In a large saucepan, bring 2 cups of almond milk and 1 cup of water to a boil.

2. Once boiling, reduce heat to low and stir in 1 cup of oats.

3. Cook for 5 minutes, stirring occasionally.

4. Add 1/4 cup of dried blueberries and stir until combined.

5. Turn off heat and let cool for 2 minutes.

6. Add a sprinkle of sliced almonds, if it's your desire.

Prep Time: 10 minutes

Lunch: Grilled salmon with quinoa and a side salad.

Preparation Time: 30 minutes

Grilled Salmon with Quinoa and a Side Salad

Ingredients:

- 4 salmon fillets, skin on

- 1 cup quinoa

- 2 tablespoons olive oil

- 1 teaspoon garlic powder

- 1 teaspoon smoked paprika

- Salt and pepper

- 4 cups mixed greens

- ½ cup chopped cherry tomatoes

- ½ cup crumbled feta cheese

- 2 tablespoons balsamic vinaigrette

Instructions:

1. Preheat the grill to medium-high heat.

2. Rinse quinoa and place in a medium saucepan with 2 cups of water. Bring to a boil, then reduce heat and simmer for 15 minutes, or until the quinoa is tender.

3. Meanwhile, brush the salmon fillets with olive oil and season with garlic powder, smoked paprika, salt and pepper.

4. Place the salmon fillets on the preheated grill and cook for 4 minutes per side, or until the salmon is cooked through.

5. In a large bowl, combine the mixed greens, cherry tomatoes and feta cheese. Drizzle with balsamic vinaigrette and toss to combine.

6. Serve the grilled salmon with the cooked quinoa and side salad. Enjoy!

Snack: Greek yogurt with honey and walnuts.

Prep time: 5 minutes

Method:

1. Begin by getting a bowl and adding one cup of plain Greek yogurt.

2. Drizzle a tablespoon of honey over the yogurt.

3. Top the yogurt with a handful of chopped walnuts.

4. Stir the ingredients together, making sure the yogurt is evenly coated with honey and walnuts.

5. Serve the Greek yogurt with honey and walnuts. Enjoy!

Dinner: Veggie stir-fry with brown rice.

Prep Time: 10 minutes

Cook Time: 15 minutes

Total Time: 25 minutes

Ingredients:
- 1 cup of brown rice
- 2 tablespoons of vegetable oil
- 2 cloves of garlic, minced
- 1 onion, diced
- 1 red bell pepper, diced
- 1 green bell pepper, diced
- 1 carrot, diced
- 1 cup of mushrooms, sliced
- 2 cups of broccoli florets
- 1 cup of snow peas
- 2 tablespoons of soy sauce
- Salt and black pepper, to taste

Instructions:

1. Cook the brown rice according to the package instructions.

2. Heat the oil in a large skillet over medium-high heat.

3. Add the garlic and onion and cook, stirring occasionally, until the onion is softened, about 3 minutes.

4. Add the bell peppers, carrot, mushrooms, and broccoli and cook, stirring occasionally, for 4 minutes.

5. Add the snow peas and cook for another minute.

6. Add the soy sauce, salt, and pepper and stir to combine.

7. Serve the stir-fry with the cooked brown rice. Enjoy!

Day 3: **Breakfast**: Avocado toast with poached eggs.

Prep Time: 15 minutes

Ingredients:

- 2 slices of whole wheat bread

- 1 large ripe avocado

- 2 eggs

- Salt and pepper

- Olive oil

- 2 slices of tomato

- Chopped parsley (optional)

Instructions:

1. Boil a pot of water.

2. Toast your slices of whole wheat bread in a toaster or a skillet over medium heat.

3. Cut your avocado in half, remove the stone and scoop out the flesh with a spoon. Mash the avocado in a bowl with a fork and season with salt and pepper.

4. Once the water is boiling, reduce the heat to low and add a teaspoon of white vinegar.

5. Crack the eggs into a small bowl, then carefully tip them into the water.

6. Use a spoon to swirl the water around the eggs for about 2 minutes until the whites are cooked.

7. Remove the eggs from the water with a slotted spoon and drain off any excess water.

8. Spread the mashed avocado on the toasted bread.

9. Top with the poached eggs and tomato slices.

10. Drizzle with olive oil and sprinkle with chopped parsley (optional).

11. Serve immediately.

Enjoy!

Lunch: Hummus wrap with greens and tomatoes.

Prep Time: 10 minutes

Servings: 1

Ingredients:

•2 whole-wheat tortillas

1/4 cup hummus

•1/2 cup baby spinach

•1/2 cup chopped tomatoes

•2 tablespoons crumbled feta cheese

•2 tablespoons chopped olives

•1 teaspoon olive oil

•Salt and pepper, to taste

Instructions:

1. Heat a large skillet over medium heat.

2. Place one tortilla in the skillet and spread hummus evenly over the top.

3. Top the hummus with spinach, tomatoes, feta cheese, and olives.

4. Drizzle the top of the wrap with olive oil and season with salt and pepper, to taste.

5. Place the other tortilla on top and press down lightly.

6. Cook for 3-4 minutes, or until the bottom tortilla is golden brown and crisp.

7. Carefully flip the wrap and cook for an additional 3-4 minutes, or until the second side is golden brown and crisp.

8. Remove from heat and slice in half. Serve warm.

Snack: Apple slices with peanut butter.

Dinner: Baked tofu with roasted veggies.

Prep Time: 15 minutes

Cook Time: 30 minutes

Total Time: 45 minutes

Ingredients:

• 14 ounces firm or extra firm tofu

• 2 tablespoons olive oil

• 1 teaspoon garlic powder

• 1 teaspoon onion powder

• 1 teaspoon paprika

• 1 teaspoon sea salt

• 2 cups of your favorite vegetables, diced (such as bell peppers, zucchini, and mushrooms)

Instructions:

1. Preheat oven to 375°F.

2. Cut the tofu into cubes and place in a large bowl.

3. Drizzle with olive oil and sprinkle with garlic powder, onion powder, paprika, and sea salt. Mix everything together until the tofu is smoothly enclosed.

4. Spread out the tofu cubes on a baking sheet.

5. Place the diced vegetables on the baking sheet next to the tofu.

6. Place the baking sheet in the oven and bake for 25-30 minutes, until the tofu is golden brown and crispy and the vegetables are tender.

7. Serve warm and enjoy!

Day 4: **Breakfast**: Scrambled eggs with spinach and mushrooms.

Prep Time: 15 minutes

Ingredients:

- 4 eggs

- 2 tablespoons of olive oil

- 1 cup of spinach

- 1/2 cup of chopped mushrooms

- Salt and pepper to taste

Instructions:

1. Crack the eggs into a bowl and whisk them until they are fully combined.

2. Heat the olive oil in a large skillet over medium-high heat.

3. Add the spinach and mushrooms to the skillet and cook for 3-4 minutes, until the vegetables are tender.

4. Pour the whisked eggs into the skillet with the vegetables and reduce the heat to medium.

5. Gently scramble the eggs and vegetables together for about 5 minutes, until the eggs are cooked through.

6. Add your salt and pepper.

7. Serve the scrambled eggs with spinach and mushrooms warm. Enjoy!

Lunch: Chicken soup with quinoa.

Prep Time: 10 minutes

Cook Time: 45 minutes

Total Time: 55 minutes

Ingredients:

• 4 cups chicken broth

- 1/2 cup quinoa, rinsed
- 2 cloves garlic, minced
- 2 tablespoons olive oil
- 2 carrots, diced
- 2 celery stalks, diced
- 1 yellow onion, diced
- 2 boneless, skinless chicken breasts, diced
- 1/4 teaspoon dried thyme
- Salt and black pepper, to taste

Instructions:

1. In a large pot, turn the heat to medium-high and add the olive oil.

2. Add the garlic, carrots, celery, and onion and sauté for 5 minutes.

3. Add the chicken and cook for another 5 minutes, or until the chicken is cooked through.

4. Pour in the chicken broth and bring it to a boil.

5. Reduce the heat to low, add the quinoa and thyme and simmer for 25 minutes.

6. Once the quinoa is cooked, season with salt and pepper and serve. Enjoy!

Snack: A handful of nuts.

Dinner: Roasted salmon with asparagus.

Prep Time: 10 minutes

Cook Time: 25 minutes

Total Time: 35 minutes

Ingredients:

-2 salmon fillets, 6-8 ounces each

-1/2 pound fresh asparagus

-2 tablespoons olive oil

-1/2 teaspoon salt

-1/4 teaspoon black pepper

-1/4 teaspoon garlic powder

-1/4 teaspoon onion powder

-1/4 teaspoon paprika

Instructions:

1. Preheat oven to 400°F.

2. Cover a baking sheet with parchment paper or aluminium foil.

3. Place the salmon fillets on the baking sheet.

4. Place the asparagus around the salmon fillets on the baking sheet.

5. Drizzle the salmon and asparagus with the olive oil.

6. Sprinkle with the salt, black pepper, garlic powder, onion powder, and paprika.

7. Roast in the preheated oven for 25 minutes, or until the salmon is cooked through and the asparagus is tender.

8. Serve warm. Enjoy!

Day 5: **Breakfast**: Smoothie made with banana, almond milk, and flaxseed.

Prep Time: 5 minutes

Servings: 1

Ingredients:

• 1 banana, peeled and sliced

• 1 cup unsweetened almond milk

• 1 tablespoon ground flaxseed

• 1/4 teaspoon ground cinnamon (optional)

• 2-3 ice cubes (optional)

Instructions:

1. Place the banana slices in a blender and blend until smooth.

2. Add the almond milk, ground flaxseed, and ground cinnamon and blend until combined.

3. Add the ice cubes and blend until desired consistency is reached.

4. Serve and enjoy!

Lunch: Turkey and vegetable wrap.

Prep Time: 10 minutes

Ingredients:

-2 (10-inch) flour tortillas

-¼ cup shredded cheddar cheese

-4 ounces thinly sliced deli turkey

-1 cup mesclun greens

-1 small tomato, chopped

-¼ cup thinly sliced red onion

-4 tablespoons ranch dressing

Instructions:

1. Place tortillas on a flat surface.

2. Sprinkle cheddar cheese over each tortilla.

3. Top with turkey, mesclun greens, tomato, and red onion.

4. Drizzle each wrap with 2 tablespoons of ranch dressing.

5. Fold up the sides of the tortillas and roll up tightly.

6. Cut the wraps in half and serve.

Snack: Greek yogurt with berries.

Dinner: Baked sweet potatoes with black beans and a side salad.

Prep Time: 10 minutes

Cook Time: 40 minutes

Total Time: 50 minutes

Ingredients:

- 2 large sweet potatoes

- 1 15-oz can black beans, drained and rinsed

- 2 tablespoons olive oil

- 1 teaspoon cumin

- ½ teaspoon garlic powder

- Salt and pepper to taste

- 1 head of lettuce

- 1 tomato, diced

- ½ cucumber, diced

- 2 tablespoons olive oil

- 1 tablespoon balsamic vinegar

Instructions:

1. Preheat oven to 400 degrees F.

2. Scrub the sweet potatoes thoroughly and puncture the skin multiple times with a fork. Place on a baking sheet and bake for 40 minutes, flipping once halfway through.

3. Meanwhile, in a medium bowl, combine the black beans, olive oil, cumin, garlic powder, salt, and pepper. Mix until everything is evenly combined.

4. Once the sweet potatoes are finished baking, let cool for about 5 minutes, then cut in half and top with the black bean mixture.

5. In a large bowl, combine the lettuce, tomato, and cucumber. Drizzle with olive oil and balsamic vinegar, and season with salt and pepper to taste.

6. Serve the baked sweet potatoes with the side salad and enjoy!

Day 6: **Breakfast**: Omelet with mushrooms, peppers, and cheese.
Prep Time: 10 minutes

Ingredients:
- 2 large eggs

- 2 tablespoons of butter

- 2 tablespoons of mushrooms, diced

- 2 tablespoons of green bell pepper, diced

- 2 tablespoons of shredded cheese

- Salt and pepper, to taste

Instructions:

1. Whisk together the eggs in a bowl. Season with salt and pepper.

2. Put the butter in a non stick pan and heat it over a medium heat until it melts.

3. Add the mushrooms and bell pepper to the pan and cook until softened, about 5 minutes.

4. Pour the eggs into the pan and let cook until the edges start to set, about 3 minutes.

5. Sprinkle the cheese over the omelet and fold in half.

6. Cook for another 2 minutes, or until the cheese is melted and the omelet is cooked through.

7. Serve hot and enjoy!

Lunch: Lentil soup with a side of vegetables.

Prep Time: 10 minutes

Cook Time: 30 minutes

Total Time: 40 minutes

Ingredients:

- 2 tablespoons olive oil
- 1 onion, chopped
- 2 cloves garlic, minced
- 2 carrots, diced
- 2 celery stalks, diced
- 1 teaspoon dried thyme
- 1 teaspoon dried oregano
- 1 teaspoon ground cumin
- 1/4 teaspoon ground cinnamon
- 1/4 teaspoon ground nutmeg
- 1 cup green lentils, rinsed
- 8 cups vegetable broth
- 2 cups diced potatoes
- 1/2 cup frozen peas
- 1/2 cup diced zucchini
- 1/2 cup diced yellow squash
- Salt and pepper to taste

Instructions:

1. Put a large pot on a stove set to medium high heat, and heat the olive oil in it.

2. Add the onion, garlic, carrots, and celery and sauté until the vegetables are softened, about 5 minutes.

3. Add the thyme, oregano, cumin, cinnamon, and nutmeg and stir to combine.

4. Add the lentils and vegetable broth, stir, and bring the mixture to a boil.

5. Reduce the heat to medium-low, cover the pot, and simmer for 20 minutes.

6. Add the potatoes, peas, zucchini, and squash and simmer for an additional 10 minutes, or until the lentils and vegetables are cooked through.

7. Season with salt and pepper to taste.

8. Serve hot.

Snack: Apple slices with almond butter.
Dinner: Baked chicken with roasted vegetables.

Ingredients:
- 4 boneless, skinless chicken breasts
- 2 tablespoons olive oil
- 1 tablespoon minced garlic
- 1 teaspoon dried oregano
- 1 teaspoon dried thyme

- 1 teaspoon salt
- ½ teaspoon black pepper
- 1 large sweet potato, cut into 1-inch cubes
- 1 red bell pepper, cut into 1-inch cubes
- 1 yellow bell pepper, cut into 1-inch cubes
- 2 cups baby carrots
- 2 tablespoons chopped fresh parsley

Instructions:

1. Preheat oven to 375 degrees F.

2. Place chicken breasts in a baking dish. Drizzle with olive oil and sprinkle with garlic, oregano, thyme, salt, and pepper.

3. In a separate bowl, mix together the sweet potato, bell peppers, and carrots.

4. Spread the vegetables around the chicken in the baking dish.

5. Bake for 35 minutes, or until the chicken is cooked through and the vegetables are tender.

6. Sprinkle with fresh parsley before serving.

Prep Time: 15 minutes
Cook Time: 35 minutes

Day 7: **Breakfast**: Overnight oats with almond milk, banana, and chia seeds.

Prep time

5 minutes

Ingredients

-1/2 cup rolled oats

-1/2 cup almond milk

-1 banana, sliced

-2 tablespoons chia seeds

Instructions

1. In a bowl, combine oats, almond milk, banana slices, and chia seeds.

2. Mix everything together until the ingredients are fully combined.

3. Place the bowl in the refrigerator overnight.

4. In the morning, remove the bowl from the refrigerator and enjoy your overnight oats with almond milk, banana, and chia seeds!

Lunch: Grilled cheese with tomato soup.

Ingredients:
2 slices of bread
2 slices of cheese
Butter
1 can of tomato soup

Preparation:
1. Heat a skillet over medium heat.
2. Butter one side of each slice of bread. Place one slice in the skillet, butter-side down. Place cheese slices on top of bread, then top with other slice of bread, butter-side up.
3. Grill until bread is golden brown and cheese is melted, about 3-4 minutes per side.
4. Meanwhile, heat up the can of tomato soup in a pot on the stove.
5. Cut grilled cheese sandwich into triangles, then serve with tomato soup.

Prep Time: 10 minutes

Snack: Celery sticks with hummus.

Dinner: Baked fish with roasted asparagus.

Prep Time: 10 minutes

Cook Time: 20 minutes

Total Time: 30 minutes

Ingredients:

• 2 fillets of white fish (such as cod or haddock)

• 2 bunches of asparagus, trimmed

• 2 tablespoons olive oil

• 1/2 teaspoon garlic powder

• 1/2 teaspoon dried oregano

• Salt and pepper to taste

Preparation:

1. Preheat oven to 375 degrees F.

2. Line a baking sheet with foil and spray with cooking spray.

3. Place fish fillets on baking sheet.

4. In a large bowl, combine asparagus, olive oil, garlic powder, oregano, salt, and pepper. Toss until asparagus is evenly coated.

5. Place asparagus on baking sheet around the fish.

6. Bake for 20 minutes, or until fish is cooked through and asparagus is tender.

7. Serve immediately. Enjoy!

Day 8: **Breakfast**: Yogurt bowl with fruit and nuts.
Prep Time: 5 minutes

Recipes:

- 1 cup plain Greek yogurt

- 1/4 cup diced fresh fruit such as strawberries, blueberries, or bananas

- 2 tablespoons chopped nuts such as almonds, walnuts, or pecans

- 2 tablespoons honey or agave nectar

- 1/4 teaspoon ground cinnamon

- A pinch of sea salt

Preparation Method:

1. In a bowl, combine the yogurt, fruit and nuts.

2. Add the honey or agave nectar, cinnamon, and salt and mix everything together.

3. Serve chilled or at room temperature. Enjoy!

Lunch: Tuna salad with avocado and cucumber.

Prep Time: 15 minutes

Ingredients:

- 2 cans of tuna
- 1 ripe avocado, diced
- 1 cucumber, diced
- 2 tablespoons of lime juice
- 2 tablespoons of olive oil
- Salt and pepper to taste

Preparation Method:

1. Drain the cans of tuna and place in a medium-sized bowl.
2. Dice the avocado and cucumber. Add them to the bowl with the tuna.
3. Add the lime juice, olive oil, salt, and pepper to the bowl.
4. Mix all of the ingredients together until well-combined.
5. Serve the tuna salad with avocado and cucumber over a bed of lettuce or in a sandwich. Enjoy!

Snack: A handful of almonds.

Dinner: Roasted vegetables with quinoa.

Prep time: 20 minutes

Recipes:
- 2 cups cooked quinoa
- 1 red pepper, diced
- 1 zucchini, diced
- 1 red onion, diced
- 2 cloves garlic, minced
- 2 tablespoons olive oil
- 1 teaspoon Italian seasoning
- Salt and pepper, to taste

Preparation method:

1. Preheat oven to 400 degrees F.

2. In a large bowl, combine the quinoa, diced red pepper, zucchini, red onion, garlic, olive oil, Italian seasoning, salt and pepper.

3. Spread the mixture onto a baking sheet and bake for 15-20 minutes, or until the vegetables are tender and lightly browned.

4. Serve warm with your favorite toppings. Enjoy!

Day 9: **Breakfast**: Avocado toast with poached eggs.

Prep Time: 10 minutes

Recipes:

- 2 slices of your favorite bread

- 1 ripe avocado

- 2 eggs

- Salt and pepper to taste

- Optional toppings: red pepper flakes, chopped cilantro, sliced tomatoes

Preparation Method:

1. Toast the bread slices in a toaster or in a skillet over medium heat until golden brown.

2. Meanwhile, peel and slice the avocado.

3. Poach the eggs in a pot of simmering water for about 3-4 minutes, or until the whites are set and the yolks are still runny.

4. Place the toasted bread on a plate and top with the avocado slices.

5. Carefully remove the poached eggs from the water with a slotted spoon and place on top of the avocado slices.

6. Sprinkle with salt and pepper to taste, and any other desired toppings.

7. Serve and enjoy!

Lunch: Lentil soup with a side of vegetables.
Prep Time: 15 minutes

Recipes:
- 1 cup green lentils
- 1 onion, diced
- 2 cloves garlic, minced
- 2 tablespoons olive oil
- 4 cups vegetable broth
- 2 carrots, diced
- 1 celery stalk, diced
- 2 teaspoons paprika
- 1 teaspoon thyme
- 1 teaspoon cumin
- 1 teaspoon black pepper
- 1 cup shredded cabbage

For the Vegetables:

- 2 tablespoons olive oil

- 1 onion, diced

- 2 cloves garlic, minced

- 2 carrots, diced

- 1 celery stalk, diced

- 2 cups sliced mushrooms

- 2 cups chopped kale

- 1 teaspoon paprika

- 1 teaspoon thyme

- 1 teaspoon cumin

- 1 teaspoon black pepper

Preparation Method:

1. Begin by heating some olive oil in a large pot over a medium flame. Once the oil is hot, add the onions and garlic and cook until softened, approximately 5 minutes.

2. Add the lentils, vegetable broth, carrots, celery, paprika, thyme, cumin, and black pepper. Bring to a boil, then reduce the heat and simmer for 15 minutes, stirring occasionally.

3. Meanwhile, heat the remaining olive oil in a large skillet over medium heat. Add the onions and garlic and cook until softened, about 5 minutes.

4. Add the carrots, celery, mushrooms, kale, paprika, thyme, cumin, and black pepper. Cook until the vegetables are tender, about 8-10 minutes.

5. Add the cooked vegetables to the soup and simmer for an additional 5 minutes. Serve with a side of shredded cabbage. Enjoy!

Snack: Greek yogurt with honey and walnuts.
Dinner: Baked salmon with roasted broccoli.
Prep Time: 15 minutes

Ingredients:
- 2 salmon fillets
- 2 cups of broccoli florets
- 2 tablespoons olive oil
- 2 tablespoons freshly squeezed lemon juice
- 2 cloves of garlic, minced
- 2 tablespoons of chopped fresh parsley
- Salt and pepper to taste

Preparation Method:

1. Preheat oven to 400 degrees F.

2. Place the salmon fillets and broccoli florets onto a baking sheet lined with parchment paper.

3. Drizzle olive oil over the salmon and broccoli and sprinkle with lemon juice, minced garlic, and chopped parsley. Add salt and pepper to taste.

4. Bake for 15 minutes, or until the salmon is cooked through and the broccoli is tender.

5. Serve and enjoy!

Day 10: **Breakfast**: Scrambled eggs with spinach and mushrooms.

Prep time: 10 minutes

Ingredients:

-3 large eggs

-1/4 cup of fresh spinach

-1/4 cup of chopped mushrooms

-1 tablespoon of butter

-Salt and pepper to taste

Preparation Method:

1. Heat a skillet over medium heat.

2. Add the butter to the skillet and let it melt.

3. Add the mushrooms and spinach and cook for a few minutes until the vegetables are softened.

4. Crack the eggs into a bowl, season with salt and pepper, and whisk until combined.

5. Pour the egg mixture into the skillet, stirring constantly as it cooks.

6. Scramble the eggs until they are cooked through, about 3 minutes.

7. Serve the scrambled eggs with spinach and mushrooms, and enjoy.

Lunch: Grilled chicken with quinoa and a side salad.
Prep time: 15 minutes

Ingredients:
-4 boneless, skinless chicken breasts
-1 cup cooked quinoa
-1/4 cup olive oil
-Salt and pepper
-Your favorite salad ingredients (lettuce, tomatoes, onions, cucumbers, etc.)

Preparation Method:

1. Turn your grill or grill pan up to a medium-high setting and allow it to preheat.

2. Rub the chicken breasts with the olive oil, salt, and pepper.

3. Place the chicken breasts on the grill and cook for 4-5 minutes per side, or until the internal temperature reaches 165F.

4. Meanwhile, prepare the quinoa according to the package instructions.

5. Assemble the salad with your favorite ingredients.

6. Serve the grilled chicken with the quinoa and side salad. Enjoy!

Snack: Apple slices with peanut butter.

Dinner: Veggie stir-fry with brown rice.

Prep Time: 10 minutes

Recipes:

- 1 cup of uncooked brown rice
- 2 tablespoons of vegetable oil
- 1/2 cup of diced onion
- 1/2 cup of diced red bell pepper

- 1/2 cup of diced zucchini

- 1/2 cup of diced carrots

- 1/2 cup of snow peas

- 1/4 cup of soy sauce

- 2 tablespoons of honey

- 2 cloves of garlic, minced

- 1/2 teaspoon of grated ginger

- Salt and pepper to taste

Preparation Method:

1. Cook the brown rice according to the instructions on the package.

2. In a large skillet, heat the oil over medium-high heat. Add the onion, bell pepper, zucchini, carrots, and snow peas. Stir-fry for 5 minutes, or until the vegetables are tender.

3. In a bowl, combine the soy sauce, honey, garlic, and ginger. Pour the mixture over the vegetables and stir-fry for 1 minute.

4. Add the cooked brown rice to the skillet and stir-fry for 2 minutes.

5. Add salt and pepper to taste,then serve.

Day 11: **Breakfast**: Smoothie made with banana, 1/2 scoop of protein powder, almond milk, and 1/2 cup of oats.

Prep Time: 5 minutes

Recipe:

Ingredients:

- 1 banana

- 1/2 scoop of protein powder

- 1/2 cup almond milk

- 1/2 cup of oats

Preparation Method:

1. Place banana, protein powder, almond milk, and oats in a blender.

2. Blend on high speed until ingredients are well combined and smooth.

3. Serve immediately and enjoy!

Lunch: Hummus wrap with greens and tomatoes.

Prep time: 15 minutes

Ingredients:

1/2 cup hummus

2 whole wheat wraps

1/2 cup baby spinach

2 small tomatoes, sliced

1/4 cup shredded carrots

1/4 cup sliced red onion

Preparation Method:

1. Put the large skillet over a stove and turn the heat to medium.

2. Spread the hummus evenly over each wrap.

3. Top each wrap with a layer of baby spinach, tomatoes, carrots, and red onion.

4. Carefully fold the wraps in half and place them in the skillet.

5. Cook for about 2 minutes on each side, or until the wraps are lightly browned and the vegetables are softened.

6. Remove from the skillet and cut each wrap in half.

7. Serve with your favorite dipping sauce. Enjoy!

Snack: A handful of nuts.

Dinner: Baked tofu with roasted veggies.

Prep Time: 30 minutes

Ingredients

- 1 block firm tofu
- 1 red bell pepper, diced
- 1 yellow bell pepper, diced
- 1 zucchini, diced
- 1 onion, diced
- 2 cloves garlic, minced
- 2 tablespoons olive oil
- 2 tablespoons soy sauce
- 2 tablespoons apple cider vinegar
- 2 tablespoons honey
- 2 teaspoons ground ginger
- Salt and pepper, to taste

Preparation Method

1. Preheat oven to 375 degrees F.

2. Drain and press the tofu to remove excess water. Cut the tofu into cubes.

3. In a large bowl, combine the bell peppers, zucchini, onion, garlic, olive oil, soy sauce, apple cider vinegar, honey, ground ginger, salt and pepper. Toss to combine.

4. Place the tofu cubes into an even layer on a baking sheet. Top with the vegetable mixture.

5. Bake for 25-30 minutes, stirring halfway through, until the tofu is golden and the vegetables are tender.

6. Serve warm and enjoy!

Day 12: Breakfast: Oatmeal with blueberries and almond milk. Prep Time: 5 minutes

Ingredients:

-1/2 cup old-fashioned rolled oats

-1 cup unsweetened almond milk

-1/4 cup fresh or frozen blueberries

-1 tablespoon honey

-1 teaspoon ground cinnamon

-1 tablespoon sliced almonds

Preparation Method:

1. In a medium saucepan over medium heat, bring the almond milk to a simmer.

2. Add the oats and stir to combine.

3. Reduce the heat to low and cook for 3-4 minutes, stirring occasionally.

4. Add the blueberries, honey and cinnamon. Stir to combine.

5. Cook for an additional 2-3 minutes until the oatmeal is creamy and the blueberries are soft.

6. Serve the oatmeal into bowls and top with the sliced almonds. Enjoy!

Lunch: Turkey and vegetable wrap.
Prep Time: 10 minutes

Recipes:
- 1 large tortilla wrap
- 2 slices of cooked turkey
- 1/4 cup of sliced bell peppers
- 1/4 cup of shredded carrots
- 1/4 cup of diced tomatoes
- 2 tablespoons of ranch dressing

Preparation Method:
1. Preheat a griddle pan over medium heat.
2. Place the tortilla wrap on the griddle and cook for 1-2 minutes until lightly toasted.

3. Remove the tortilla from the heat and place on a plate.

4. Layer the cooked turkey, bell peppers, carrots, tomatoes, and ranch dressing on one half of the tortilla.

5. Fold the other half of the tortilla over the filling and press down lightly.

6. Return the wrap to the griddle and cook for 2-3 minutes until lightly browned and the filling is heated through.

7. Cut the wrap into two and dish out. Enjoy!

Snack: Greek yogurt with berries.

Dinner: Baked sweet potatoes with black beans and a side salad.

Prep Time: 10 minutes

Recipes:
- 2 medium sweet potatoes, peeled and cubed
- 1/2 cup black beans, drained and rinsed
- 1/4 cup diced red onion
- 1/4 cup diced bell pepper
- 2 tablespoons olive oil
- 1 teaspoon cumin

- 1 teaspoon chili powder

- 1/2 teaspoon garlic powder

- 1/4 teaspoon salt

- 1/4 teaspoon black pepper

- Side salad of your choice

Preparation Method:

1. Preheat oven to 400 degrees F.

2. In a large bowl, combine sweet potatoes, black beans, red onion, bell pepper, olive oil, cumin, chili powder, garlic powder, salt, and black pepper. Mix until everything is evenly coated.

3. Transfer the mixture to a greased baking dish.

4. Bake for 12 minutes, then stir and bake for an additional 13 minutes.

5. Serve hot with a side salad. Enjoy!

Day 13: **Breakfast**: Avocado toast with poached eggs. Prep Time: 10 minutes

Ingredients:

- 2 slices of bread

- 1 avocado

- 2 eggs

- Salt and pepper to taste

- Optional: red pepper flakes

Instructions:

1. Heat a pot of water until it reaches a boiling point.

2. Toast your bread in a toaster or toaster oven.

3. Split the avocado in two, take out the seed and scoop out the inside. Mash the avocado with a fork in a small bowl and season with salt and pepper to taste.

4. Once water is boiling, reduce heat to low and add the eggs. Poach for 4 minutes.

5. Spread the mashed avocado on each slice of toast.

6. Remove the poached eggs from the water and place on top of the avocado.

7. Sprinkle with salt, pepper, and optional red pepper flakes. Enjoy!

Lunch: Chicken soup with quinoa.

Prep Time: 15 minutes

Ingredients:

- 1 tablespoon olive oil

- 1 onion, diced

- 2 cloves garlic, minced

- 2 carrots, diced

- 2 celery stalks, diced

- 4 cups chicken broth

- 1/2 cup quinoa, rinsed

- 1/4 teaspoon dried thyme

- 1/4 teaspoon dried oregano

- 1 bay leaf

- 1/2 teaspoon sea salt

- 1/4 teaspoon freshly ground black pepper

- 2 cups cooked, shredded chicken

- 2 tablespoons freshly chopped parsley

Preparation Method:

1. In a large pot, heat the olive oil over medium flames. Add the onion, garlic, carrots, and celery and sauté for 5 minutes.

2. Add the chicken broth, quinoa, thyme, oregano, bay leaf, salt, and pepper to the pot and bring to a boil. Reduce the heat to low and simmer, covered, for 15 minutes, stirring occasionally.

3. Add the cooked chicken and parsley to the pot and stir to combine. Cook for an additional 2-3 minutes, until the chicken is heated through.

4. Serve the soup warm. Enjoy!

Snack: Celery sticks with hummus.

Dinner: Roasted salmon with asparagus.

Prep Time: 15 minutes

Cook Time: 20 minutes

Total Time: 35 minutes

Servings: 4

Ingredients:

• 1 ½ lbs. salmon, cut into 4 fillets

• 1 lb. asparagus, trimmed and cut into 2-inch pieces

• 2 tablespoons olive oil

• 1 teaspoon dried oregano

• Salt and pepper, to taste

• 2 tablespoons freshly squeezed lemon juice

• 2 tablespoons chopped fresh parsley

Instructions:

1. Preheat oven to 400°F.

2. Place the salmon fillets on a baking sheet lined with parchment paper.

3. In a large bowl, combine the asparagus, olive oil, oregano, salt, and pepper. Toss to combine.

4. Arrange the asparagus around the salmon fillets.

5. Bake for 20 minutes, or until the salmon is cooked through and the asparagus is tender.

6. Sprinkle with lemon juice and parsley before serving.

Day 14: **Breakfast**: Scrambled eggs with spinach and mushrooms. Prep Time: 10 minutes

Ingredients:
- 2 eggs
- 2 tablespoons of butter
- 1/4 cup of chopped mushrooms
- 1/4 cup of chopped spinach
- 1/4 cup of shredded cheese
- Salt and pepper

Preparation:

1. In a medium bowl, whisk together the eggs until they are completely blended.

2. In a large skillet, melt the butter over medium heat.

3. Add the mushrooms and spinach and cook for 5 minutes, stirring occasionally.

4. Reduce the heat to low and add the eggs, stirring constantly.

5. When the eggs are almost cooked, add the cheese and stir to combine.

6. Add salt and pepper to taste.

7. Serve immediately.

Lunch: Grilled salmon with quinoa and a side salad. Prep Time: 15 minutes

Ingredients:

-4 salmon fillets

-1 cup cooked quinoa

-1/4 cup olive oil

-2 tablespoons lemon juice

-Salt and pepper to taste

-1/4 cup chopped parsley

-1/4 cup chopped mint

-1/4 cup chopped scallions

-1/4 cup crumbled feta cheese

-1 head romaine lettuce, torn into pieces

-1/2 cucumber, sliced

Instructions:

1. Preheat a grill to medium-high heat.

2. Brush the salmon fillets with olive oil, lemon juice, salt and pepper.

3. Place the salmon fillets on the preheated grill and cook for 4-5 minutes per side, or until the salmon is cooked through.

4. Meanwhile, in a medium bowl, combine the cooked quinoa, parsley, mint, scallions, and feta cheese.

5. In a large bowl, combine the lettuce and cucumber.

6. Drizzle the lettuce and cucumber with the remaining olive oil, lemon juice, salt and pepper, and toss to combine.

7. Serve the salmon with the quinoa and side salad. Enjoy!

Snack: Apple slices with almond butter.

Dinner: Baked chicken with roasted vegetables.

Prep time: 20 minutes

Ingredients:

-3 chicken breasts

-2 cloves of garlic, minced

-1/2 teaspoon of dried oregano

-1/2 teaspoon of dried thyme

-1/4 teaspoon of salt

-1/4 teaspoon of pepper

-1/4 cup of olive oil

-2 bell peppers, sliced

-1 onion, sliced

-2 carrots, chopped

-2 potatoes, chopped

Preparation Method:

1. Preheat the oven to 350°F.

2. In a small bowl, mix together the garlic, oregano, thyme, salt and pepper. Rub the mixture onto the chicken breasts.

3. Put the olive oil in a large safe skillet over a medium heat. Add the chicken breasts and cook

until lightly browned, about 3 minutes per side. Remove the chicken and set aside.

4. Add the bell peppers, onion, carrots, and potatoes to the skillet and cook until vegetables are lightly browned, about 5 minutes.

5. Place the chicken breasts on top of the vegetables and transfer the skillet to the preheated oven. Bake for 15 minutes, or until chicken is cooked through.

6. Serve the baked chicken with roasted vegetables. Enjoy!

Day 15: **Breakfast**: Smoothie made with banana, almond milk, and flaxseed.
Prep time: 5 minutes

Ingredients:
- 1 banana
- 1 cup almond milk
- 1 tablespoon flaxseed

Preparation Method:
1. Remove the skin from the banana and cut into small pieces.

2. Place banana pieces in a blender.

3. Add almond milk and flaxseed and blend until smooth.

4. Serve in a glass and enjoy!

Lunch: Tuna salad with avocado and cucumber.
Prep time: 10 minutes

Ingredients:
- 2 cans of tuna
- 1 avocado, peeled and diced
- 1 cucumber, peeled and diced
- 1/4 cup of diced red onion
- 2 tablespoons of olive oil
- 2 tablespoons of apple cider vinegar
- Salt and pepper to taste

Instructions:
1. Drain the cans of tuna and place in a large bowl.

2. Add the diced avocado, cucumber and red onion to the bowl.

3. In a separate bowl, whisk together the olive oil, apple cider vinegar, salt and pepper.

4. Pour the dressing over the tuna salad and mix until everything is evenly distributed.

5. Serve the tuna salad with avocado and cucumber chilled. Enjoy!

Snack: A handful of almonds.

Dinner: Roasted vegetables with quinoa.

Prep Time: 15 minutes

Cook Time: 30 minutes

Total Time: 45 minutes

Ingredients:

- 2 cups quinoa
- 2 bell peppers, chopped
- 2 carrots, chopped
- 2 zucchinis, chopped
- 1 onion, chopped
- 2 tablespoons olive oil
- 1 teaspoon garlic powder
- 1 teaspoon oregano
- 1 teaspoon thyme
- 1 teaspoon rosemary
- Salt and pepper, to taste

Preparation Method:

1. Set the oven to 375 degrees F.

2. Follow the directions on the quinoa package to prepare it.

3. In a large bowl, combine the bell peppers, carrots, zucchini, onion, olive oil, garlic powder, oregano, thyme, rosemary, salt, and pepper. Toss until vegetables are evenly coated.

4. Spread the vegetables on a baking sheet, and roast for 30 minutes, stirring halfway through.

5. When the vegetables are done, remove from the oven and serve over the quinoa. Enjoy!

Day 16: **Breakfast**: Overnight oats with almond milk, banana, and chia seeds.

Prep Time: 10 minutes

Ingredients:
- 1/2 cup old-fashioned oats
- 1/2 cup almond milk
- 1/2 banana, sliced
- 1 tablespoon chia seeds
- pinch of salt
- 1/2 teaspoon honey

• 1/4 teaspoon ground cinnamon

Preparation Method:

1. In a bowl, combine oats, almond milk, banana slices, chia seeds, and salt. Stir until evenly combined.

2. Cover the bowl and refrigerate overnight.

3. In the morning, stir in honey and cinnamon.

4. Serve the oats chilled, or warm them up in the microwave for 1-2 minutes before serving. Enjoy!

Lunch: Chicken salad with feta cheese, tomatoes, and cucumbers.

Prep Time: 10 minutes

Recipe:

Ingredients:

- 2 cups cooked chicken, cubed

- 1/2 cup feta cheese, crumbled

- 1/2 cup tomatoes, diced

- 1/2 cup cucumbers, diced

- 1/4 cup red onion, diced

- 1/4 cup olive oil

- 2 tablespoons lemon juice

- 1/4 teaspoon garlic powder

- Salt and pepper, to taste

Preparation Method:

1. In a large bowl, combine chicken, feta, tomatoes, cucumbers and red onion.

2. In a separate bowl, whisk together olive oil, lemon juice, garlic powder, salt, and pepper.

3. Pour the chicken mixture into the dressing and mix together.

4. Keep in the refrigerator for a minimum of 30 minutes prior to consuming. Enjoy!

Snack: Greek yogurt with honey and walnuts.
Prep Time: 15 minutes

Ingredients:

- 2 cups plain Greek yogurt

- 2 tablespoons honey

- 1/4 cup walnuts, chopped

Preparation Method:

1. In a medium bowl, combine the Greek yogurt and honey and stir until evenly combined.

2. Add the chopped walnuts and stir until everything is evenly distributed.

3. Serve the Greek yogurt with honey and walnuts in individual bowls or on top of toast or crackers. Enjoy!

Dinner: Baked fish with roasted broccoli.

Prep time: 15 minutes

Ingredients:

- 2 fish fillets

- 1 head of broccoli, cut into florets

- 2 tablespoons olive oil

- 2 tablespoons lemon juice

- Salt and pepper to taste

- 2 teaspoons minced garlic

Preparation Method:

1. Set the oven to 400 degrees F (200 degrees C).

2. Place fish fillets on a greased baking sheet.

3. In a medium bowl, combine broccoli florets, olive oil, lemon juice, salt, pepper and garlic. Toss to combine.

4. Arrange broccoli around fish on baking sheet.

5. Bake in preheated oven for 25 minutes, or until fish is cooked through and broccoli is tender.

6. Serve and enjoy!

Day 17: **Breakfast**: Yogurt bowl with fruit and nuts.
Prep Time: 10 minutes

Ingredients:
-1 cup plain Greek yogurt
-1/2 cup fresh fruit of your choice (berries, banana, etc.)
-1/4 cup chopped nuts (almonds, walnuts, etc.)
-1 tablespoon honey or maple syrup
-1/4 teaspoon cinnamon

Preparation Method:
1. In a medium bowl, combine the yogurt, fruit, nuts, honey or syrup, and cinnamon.
2. Mix until everything is evenly combined.

3. If serving right away, do so immediately; otherwise, store in the refrigerator for up to an hour before serving.

4. Enjoy!

Lunch: Grilled cheese with tomato soup.

Prep Time: 15 minutes

Recipes:

- 8 slices of white bread

- 4 tablespoons of butter

- 4 slices of cheese

- 2 cups of tomato soup

Preparation Method:

1. Preheat the oven to 350 degrees.

2. Apply butter to one side of each piece of the bread.

3. Place four slices of bread, butter side down, on a greased baking sheet.

4. Place a slice of cheese on each slice of bread.

5. Place the remaining slices of bread on top of the cheese, butter side up.

6. Bake in preheated oven for 10 minutes, or until golden brown.

7. Heat the tomato soup in a small saucepan over low heat.

8. Serve the grilled cheese with a bowl of tomato soup.

Snack: A handful of nuts.

Dinner: Baked tofu with roasted veggies.

Prep Time: 15 minutes

Cook Time: 45 minutes

Total Time: 1 hour

Ingredients:

-1 block of firm tofu, drained, pressed, and cubed

-2 cups of chopped vegetables of your choice (i.e. bell peppers, onions, mushrooms, etc.)

-2 tablespoons of olive oil

-1 teaspoon of garlic powder

-1 teaspoon of dried oregano

-1 teaspoon of dried basil

-Salt and pepper, to taste

Instructions:

1. Preheat oven to 375°F.

2. Line a baking sheet with parchment paper and spread the cubed tofu.

3. Drizzle the olive oil over the tofu and sprinkle with garlic powder, oregano, basil, salt and pepper.

4. Put the baking sheet in the oven and cook for 20 minutes.

5. Meanwhile, in a separate bowl, toss the chopped vegetables in olive oil, garlic powder, oregano, basil, salt and pepper.

6. After 20 minutes, remove the baking sheet from the oven and add the vegetables to it.

7. Return the baking sheet to the oven and bake for an additional 25 minutes, or until the vegetables are cooked through and the tofu is golden brown.

8. Serve hot and enjoy!

Day 18: **Breakfast**: Omelet with mushrooms, peppers, and cheese.
Prep Time: 10 minutes

Ingredients:
- 4 eggs

- 1/4 cup mushrooms, chopped

- 1/4 cup bell peppers, chopped

- 1/4 cup cheddar cheese, grated

- 2 tablespoons olive oil

- Salt and pepper, to taste

Preparation Method:

1. Pur the olive oil in a skillet over medium heat.

2. Add the mushrooms and bell peppers, season with salt and pepper, and cook for 3 to 4 minutes.

3. In a bowl, beat the eggs until they are light and fluffy.

4. Pour the eggs into the skillet with the vegetables, and cook for 2 to 3 minutes.

5. Sprinkle the cheese over the omelet and cook until the cheese melts.

6. Flip the omelet over and cook for another 2 minutes, or until it is cooked through.

7. Serve the omelet hot. Enjoy!

Lunch: Hummus wrap with greens and tomatoes.
Prep Time: 10 minutes

Recipes:

-2 whole wheat wraps

-1/2 cup Hummus

-1/2 cup mixed greens

-2 tomatoes, sliced

-1/4 cup feta cheese

Preparation Method:

1. Preheat a skillet over medium heat.

2. Spread the hummus evenly over the wrap.

3. Top with mixed greens, tomatoes, and feta cheese.

4. Place the wrap in the preheated skillet and cook for 2-3 minutes, or until lightly browned and crisp.

5. Carefully flip the wrap over and cook for an additional 2-3 minutes.

6. Slice the wrap into thirds and serve.

Snack: Celery sticks with hummus.

Prep time: 10 minutes

Ingredients:

3-4 celery stalks, cut into 4-inch sticks

1/2 cup hummus

Preparation Method:

1. Wash and cut the celery stalks into 4-inch sticks.

2. Place the celery sticks on a plate.

3. In a separate bowl, mix the hummus until it is creamy and spreadable.

4. Spread the hummus onto the celery sticks.

5. Serve the celery sticks with hummus and enjoy!

Dinner: Veggie stir-fry with brown rice.

Prep Time: 15 minutes

Recipes:
- 1/2 cup uncooked brown rice
- 2 tablespoons vegetable oil
- 2 cloves garlic, minced
- 1 small onion, diced
- 1 red bell pepper, diced
- 1 cup broccoli florets
- 1 cup sliced mushrooms
- 1/2 cup snow peas
- 1/4 cup soy sauce
- 2 tablespoons brown sugar
- 1/4 teaspoon ground ginger

- 1/4 teaspoon red pepper flakes

Preparation Method:

1. Follow the instructions on the package to prepare the brown rice.

2. Heat the vegetable oil in a large skillet or wok over medium heat. Add the garlic, onion, bell pepper, broccoli, mushrooms, and snow peas to the pan. Cook, stirring occasionally, until the vegetables are tender, about 5 minutes.

3. In a small bowl, combine the soy sauce, brown sugar, ginger, and red pepper flakes. Pour the mixture over the vegetables and stir to combine.

4. Cook for an additional 3-5 minutes, until the sauce is thick and bubbly.

5. Pour the stir-fry onto the cooked brown rice. Enjoy!

Day 19: **Breakfast**: Avocado toast with poached eggs.

Prep Time: 10 minutes

Ingredients:
- 2 slices of whole wheat bread

- 1/2 of an avocado
- 2 eggs
- Sea salt and freshly ground pepper, to taste
- Optional: red pepper flakes, to taste
- Optional: 2 tablespoons of crumbled feta cheese

Preparation Method:

1. Bring a small pot of water to a simmer.

2. Toast two slices of whole wheat bread.

3. Slice the avocado and spread it onto the toast.

4. Carefully crack two eggs into the simmering water and poach them for 3-4 minutes.

5. Remove the eggs with a slotted spoon and place them on top of the avocado toast.

6. Season the poached eggs with sea salt, freshly ground pepper, and optional red pepper flakes.

7. Optionally, top with crumbled feta cheese.

8. Enjoy your avocado toast with poached eggs!

Lunch: Lentil soup with a side of vegetables.
Prep Time: 10 minutes

Ingredients:

- 2 tablespoons olive oil

- 1 onion, diced

- 2 cloves garlic, minced

- 2 carrots, diced

- 1 celery stalk, diced

- 1 teaspoon dried oregano

- 1 teaspoon dried basil

- 2 cups dried lentils

- 5 cups vegetable broth

- 1 can diced tomatoes

- 1/2 teaspoon salt

- 1/4 teaspoon pepper

- 2 cups assorted vegetables (e.g. bell peppers, mushrooms, zucchini, etc.)

Preparation Method:

1. Heat the oil in a large pot over medium heat.

2. Add the onion, garlic, carrots, and celery and cook until softened, about 5 minutes.

3. Add the oregano and basil and stir to combine.

4. Add the lentils, broth, tomatoes, salt, and pepper and bring to a boil.

5. Turn the heat to low, put a lid on the pot, and cook for 20 minutes.

6. Add the vegetables and cook for an additional 10 minutes.

7. Serve hot.

Snack: Apple slices with peanut butter.

Dinner: Baked salmon with asparagus.

Prep Time: 10 minutes

Cook Time: 25 minutes

Total Time: 35 minutes

Serves: 4

Ingredients:

• 1 lb salmon

• 1 lb asparagus

• 1 lemon, sliced

• 2 tablespoons olive oil

• 1 teaspoon garlic powder

• Salt and pepper to taste

Preparation Method:

1. Preheat oven to 400 degrees F.

2. Line a baking sheet with aluminum foil and lightly grease with olive oil.

3. Place the salmon and asparagus on the baking sheet.

4. Drizzle the olive oil over the salmon and asparagus.

5. Sprinkle garlic powder, salt, and pepper over the salmon and asparagus.

6. Arrange the lemon slices on top of the salmon and asparagus.

7. Bake for 20-25 minutes, or until the salmon is cooked through and the asparagus is tender.

8. Serve and enjoy!

Day 20: **Breakfast**: Scrambled eggs with spinach and mushrooms.

Prep time: 10 - 15 minutes

Ingredients:

- 2 large eggs

- 2 tablespoons of butter

- 2 cups of spinach

- ¼ cup of diced mushrooms

- Salt and pepper to taste

Preparation Method:

1. In a medium bowl, whisk the two eggs until they are light and fluffy.

2. Put the butter into the large skillet and turn the heat up to medium.

3. Once the butter has melted, add the spinach and mushrooms. Cook for 2-3 minutes until the vegetables have softened.

4. Add the whisked eggs to the skillet and season with salt and pepper.

5. Stir the eggs constantly for about 5 minutes until they are cooked through.

6. Serve the scrambled eggs with spinach and mushrooms. Enjoy!

Lunch: Turkey and vegetable wrap.
Prep Time: 10 minutes

Recipes:
-1 turkey wrap
-1/4 cup chopped lettuce
-1/4 cup chopped tomatoes
-1/4 cup grated carrots
-1/4 cup sliced cucumber

-2 tablespoons ranch dressing

Preparation Method:

1. Place the wrap on a plate.

2. Spread the ranch dressing evenly over the wrap.

3. Add the lettuce, tomatoes, carrots, and cucumber in the center of the wrap.

4. Roll the wrap up tightly, tucking in the ends.

5. Cut the wrap in half and serve.

Snack: Greek yogurt with berries.

Dinner: Baked sweet potatoes with black beans and a side salad.

Prep Time: 20 minutes

Ingredients:

2 sweet potatoes

1 can black beans, drained and rinsed

1 tablespoon olive oil

1 teaspoon chili powder

1/4 teaspoon ground cumin

Salt and pepper

For the salad:

1 head of romaine lettuce, chopped

1/2 cup cherry tomatoes, halved

1/4 cup red onion, diced

1/4 cup crumbled feta cheese

1/4 cup sliced almonds

For the dressing:

1/4 cup olive oil

2 tablespoons red wine vinegar

1 teaspoon honey

1/2 teaspoon Dijon mustard

Preparation Method:

1. Set the oven to 400 degrees F.

2. Wash and scrub the sweet potatoes and poke a few holes in each one with a fork. Place the potatoes on a baking sheet and bake for 45 minutes, or until soft when pierced with a fork.

3. In a medium bowl, combine the black beans, olive oil, chili powder, cumin, salt and pepper. Mix until everything is evenly combined.

4. When the potatoes are done baking, remove from the oven and let cool for a few minutes. Cut

each potato in half lengthwise and top with the black bean mixture.

5. Meanwhile, prepare the salad. In a large bowl, combine the lettuce, tomatoes, red onion, feta cheese and almonds.

6. In a small bowl, whisk together the olive oil, red wine vinegar, honey and Dijon mustard.

7. Drizzle the salad with the dressing and toss to combine.

8. Serve the sweet potatoes with the side salad. Enjoy!

Day 21: **Breakfast**: Oatmeal with blueberries and almond milk.
Prep time: 5 minutes

Ingredients:
-1 cup of rolled oats
-1 cup of unsweetened almond milk
-1/2 cup of fresh or frozen blueberries
-1 tablespoon of maple syrup
-1 tablespoon of chopped almonds
-1 teaspoon of cinnamon

Preparation Method:

1. In a medium saucepan, bring the almond milk to a low boil.

2. Add the rolled oats and re guy duce the heat to a simmer.

3. Cook for about 3 minutes, stirring occasionally.

4. Add the blueberries, maple syrup, almonds, and cinnamon and stir until combined.

5. Cook for 1 more minute or until the oatmeal is creamy.

6. Serve hot and enjoy!

Lunch: Grilled salmon with quinoa and a side salad.

Prep Time: 15 minutes

Recipes:

Grilled Salmon

- 4 salmon fillets

- 2 tablespoons olive oil

- 2 tablespoons lemon juice

- Salt and pepper to taste

Quinoa

- 1 cup quinoa

- 2 cups water

- 1 tablespoon olive oil

- Salt and pepper to taste

Side Salad

- 2 cups greens (arugula, spinach, etc)

- 1/2 cup cherry tomatoes, halved

- 1/4 cup feta cheese, crumbled

- 1/4 cup red onion, diced

- 2 tablespoons olive oil

- 2 tablespoons balsamic vinegar

- Salt and pepper to taste

Preparation Method:

1. Preheat the grill to medium-high heat.

2. Mix together the olive oil, lemon juice, salt, and pepper in a small bowl. Brush the salmon with the mixture.

3. Place the salmon on the preheated grill and cook for 4-5 minutes per side, or until cooked through.

4. In a medium saucepan, mix together the quinoa and water. Place on the stove, turn the heat to high,

and allow the mixture to come to a boil. Lower the heat to a simmer and cook for 15 minutes, or until the quinoa has become tender.

5. Remove the salmon from the grill and set aside.

6. In a large bowl, combine the greens, cherry tomatoes, feta cheese, and red onion.

7. Whisk together the olive oil, balsamic vinegar, salt, and pepper in a small bowl. Drizzle over the salad and toss to combine.

8. To serve, divide the quinoa among four plates and top with the grilled salmon. Serve with the side salad. Enjoy!

Snack: A handful of almonds.

Dinner: Roasted vegetables with quinoa.

Prep time: 15 minutes

Cook time: 25 minutes

Total time: 40 minutes

Ingredients:
• 2 cups of cooked quinoa
• 2 bell peppers, diced
• 2 medium carrots, diced
• 2 zucchini, diced

- 2 tablespoons of olive oil
- 2 cloves of garlic, minced
- 1 teaspoon of dried oregano
- Salt and pepper, to taste
- 1/4 cup of freshly chopped parsley
- 1/2 cup of freshly grated Parmesan cheese
- 1/4 cup of toasted pine nuts (optional)

Preparation Method:

1. Preheat oven to 375°F.

2. Spread the diced vegetables on a baking sheet and drizzle with olive oil. Sprinkle with garlic, oregano, salt, and pepper.

3. Roast the vegetables in the oven for 25 minutes, stirring once halfway through.

4. In a large bowl, combine the cooked quinoa and roasted vegetables.

5. Sprinkle with parsley, Parmesan cheese, and toasted pine nuts (if using).

6. Serve warm.

Day 22: **Breakfast**: Smoothie made with banana, almond milk, and flaxseed.
Prep time: 5 minutes

Recipes:
- 1 banana, peeled and sliced
- 1 cup almond milk
- 2 tablespoons ground flaxseed

Preparation Method:
1. Place the banana slices and almond milk into a blender and blend until smooth.
2. Add the ground flaxseed and blend again until combined.
3. Transfer the smoothie into a glass and enjoy.

Lunch: Chicken salad with feta cheese, tomatoes, and cucumbers.
Prep Time: 15 minutes

Ingredients:
- 2 cups cooked chicken, shredded
- 2 cups feta cheese, crumbled
- 2 cups tomatoes, diced

- 2 cups cucumbers, diced

- 1/4 cup fresh parsley, chopped

- 2 tablespoons olive oil

- 2 tablespoons red wine vinegar

- Salt and pepper to taste

Preparation Method:

1. In a large bowl, combine the cooked chicken, feta cheese, tomatoes, cucumbers, and parsley.

2. In a small bowl, whisk together the olive oil, red wine vinegar, salt, and pepper.

3. Pour the dressing over the chicken mixture and toss to combine.

4. Serve immediately or chill in the refrigerator until ready to serve. Enjoy!

Snack: Apple slices with almond butter.

Dinner: Baked fish with roasted broccoli.

Prep Time: 15 minutes

Cook Time: 30 minutes

Total Time: 45 minutes

Ingredients:

- 2 fillets of white fish (cod, halibut or haddock)

- 2 cups of broccoli florets
- 2 tablespoons of olive oil
- 1 tablespoon of garlic powder
- 1 tablespoon of dried oregano
- Salt and pepper to taste

Instructions:

1. Preheat oven to 375°F.

2. Cover a baking sheet with parchment paper and put it aside.

3. Place the fish fillets on the parchment paper and season with salt and pepper.

4. In a bowl, mix together the broccoli florets, olive oil, garlic powder, oregano, and salt and pepper.

5. Place the seasoned broccoli on the baking sheet around the fish.

6. Bake in the preheated oven for 30 minutes or until the fish is cooked through and the broccoli is lightly browned.

7. Serve with your favorite sides and enjoy!

Day 23: **Breakfast**: Yogurt bowl with fruit and nuts.
 Prep time: 10 minutes

Ingredients:

- 1 cup of plain Greek yogurt

- 1/2 cup of fresh fruit (your choice)

- 1/4 cup of nuts (your choice)

- 1 tablespoon of honey (optional)

Preparation Method:

1. Place the yogurt into a medium bowl.

2. Top the yogurt with the fresh fruit of your choice.

3. Sprinkle the nuts of your choice on top.

4. Drizzle the honey on top of the yogurt bowl (optional).

5. Enjoy your yogurt bowl with fruit and nuts!

Lunch: Tuna salad with avocado and cucumber.

Prep Time: 15 minutes

Ingredients:

-2 cans of tuna, drained

-1 avocado, diced

-1 cucumber, diced

-1/4 cup of chopped fresh parsley

-juice of 1 lemon

-2 tablespoons of olive oil

-Salt and pepper to taste

Preparation Method:

1. In a bowl, combine the tuna, avocado, cucumber and parsley.
2. In a separate bowl, mix together the lemon juice, olive oil, salt and pepper.
3. Pour the dressing over the tuna mixture and stir to combine.
4. Serve chilled or at room temperature.

Snack: A handful of nuts.

Dinner: Baked tofu with roasted veggies.

Prep Time: 15 minutes

Cook Time: 30 minutes

Total Time: 45 minutes

Ingredients:

-1 package of extra-firm tofu, drained and cubed

-2 tablespoons of olive oil

-1 bell pepper, chopped

-1 onion, chopped

-1 zucchini, chopped

-1 clove of garlic, minced

-1 teaspoon of dried oregano

-1 teaspoon of dried basil

-1 teaspoon of dried thyme

-Salt and pepper to taste

-1/4 cup of vegetable broth

-1/4 cup of balsamic vinegar

-2 tablespoons of maple syrup

-1/4 cup of breadcrumbs

-2 tablespoons of nutritional yeast

-1/4 cup of chopped parsley

Instructions:

1. Set your oven to 350 degrees F before baking.

2. In a large bowl, combine the cubed tofu, bell pepper, onion, zucchini, garlic, oregano, basil, thyme, salt and pepper.

3. Drizzle the olive oil over the tofu and vegetables, and mix until everything is evenly coated.

4. Spread the tofu and vegetables onto a baking sheet and bake for 25-30 minutes, or until the vegetables are tender and the tofu is golden brown.

5. Meanwhile, in a medium bowl, whisk together the vegetable broth, balsamic vinegar, maple syrup, breadcrumbs, nutritional yeast, and parsley.

6. Remove the baking sheet from the oven and pour the sauce over the tofu and vegetables.

7. Return the baking sheet to the oven and bake for an additional 5-10 minutes, or until the sauce is bubbling and the tofu is golden.

8. Serve the tofu and vegetables with your favorite sides. Enjoy!

Day 24: **Breakfast**: Omelet with mushrooms, peppers, and cheese.
Prep Time: 10 minutes

Ingredients:
- 2 eggs
- 2 tablespoons of butter
- 1/4 cup mushrooms, diced
- 1/4 cup bell peppers, diced
- 1/4 cup cheese, grated

Preparation Method:
1. Beat the eggs in a bowl until well combined.

2. Heat the butter in a skillet over medium heat.

3. Add the mushrooms and bell peppers to the skillet and sauté for about 3 minutes.

4. Pour the eggs into the skillet, and spread the vegetables evenly.

5. Sprinkle the cheese over the omelet.

6. Cook the omelet until the eggs are set, about 4 minutes.

7. Flip the omelet and cook for another 2 minutes.

8. Serve the omelet hot with your favorite sides. Enjoy!

Lunch: Grilled cheese with tomato soup.
Prep time: 10 minutes

Ingredients:
-4 slices of bread
-4 slices of cheese
-4 slices of tomato
-1/4 cup butter
-1 can of tomato soup

Preparation:

1. Preheat a skillet or griddle to medium-high heat.

2. Butter one side of each slice of bread and place them butter-side down in the skillet.

3. Place a slice of cheese and a slice of tomato on two of the slices of bread.

4. Place the remaining two slices of bread on top of the cheese and tomato to form sandwiches.

5. Grill the sandwiches for 2-3 minutes per side, or until the cheese is melted and the bread is golden brown.

6. Meanwhile, heat the tomato soup in a small saucepan over medium heat until it's hot and bubbly.

7. Enjoy the grilled cheese sandwiches served with the tomato soup!

Snack: Greek yogurt with honey and walnuts.

Dinner: Roasted salmon with asparagus.

Prep Time: 10 minutes

Cook Time: 20 minutes

Ingredients:

- 1 lb. salmon

- 2 bunches of asparagus
- 2 tablespoons olive oil
- Salt and pepper to taste

Preparation Method:

1. Preheat oven to 375°F.

2. Cover a baking sheet with parchment paper.

3. Put the salmon onto the baking sheet.

4. Drizzle olive oil over the salmon and season with salt and pepper.

5. Place the asparagus around the salmon.

6. Drizzle olive oil over the asparagus and season with salt and pepper.

7. Roast for 20 minutes, or until salmon is cooked through and asparagus is tender.

8. Enjoy your meal with your favorite side dish!

Day 25: **Breakfast**: Avocado toast with poached eggs.
Prep Time: 10 minutes

Ingredients:
- 2 slices of toast
- 2 avocados, sliced

- 2 eggs
- Salt and pepper, to taste
- Olive oil

Preparation Method:

1. Boil a pot of water.

2. Toast the bread slices in a toaster or in a skillet over medium heat.

3. Slice the avocados and spread them on the toast slices.

4. Once the water is boiling, reduce the heat to low and add a splash of white vinegar. Carefully crack the eggs into the water and poach until the whites are set and the yolks are still soft (about 3 minutes).

5. Using a slotted spoon, carefully remove the eggs from the water and place them on top of the avocado toast slices.

6. Drizzle the toast with olive oil and season with salt and pepper, to taste. Serve immediately.

Lunch: Lentil soup with a side of vegetables.
Prep Time: 20 Minutes

Ingredients:

-1 cup dry lentils

-2 cups diced carrots

-2 cups diced celery

-1 medium onion, diced

-1 teaspoon garlic powder

-2 tablespoons olive oil

-4 cups vegetable broth

-1 teaspoon fresh rosemary

-1 teaspoon fresh thyme

-Salt and pepper to taste

Vegetable Side:

-1 cup diced bell peppers

-1 cup diced zucchini

-1 cup diced squash

-1 tablespoon olive oil

-1 teaspoon garlic powder

-Salt and pepper to taste

Preparation Method:

1. Rinse the lentils and set aside.

2. Begin by heating olive oil in a large pot over medium heat. Once the oil is hot, add the onion,

carrots, and celery and cook for about 5 minutes, or until the vegetables are softened.

3. Add the garlic powder, rosemary, and thyme, and cook for another minute.

4. Put the lentils and vegetable broth in a pot, and bring to a boil. Then, lower the heat and let the mixture simmer for 15 minutes or until the lentils are fully cooked.

5. While the lentils are cooking, prepare the vegetable side. Place a large skillet on medium heat and add the olive oil to it. Add the bell peppers, zucchini, and squash, and cook until the vegetables are tender, about 5 minutes.

6. Add the garlic powder, and season with salt and pepper.

7. Serve the lentil soup with the vegetable side. Enjoy!

Snack: Celery sticks with hummus.

Dinner: Baked chicken with roasted vegetables.

Prep Time: 15 minutes

Ingredients:

-4-6 chicken breasts

-1 red bell pepper

-1 orange bell pepper

-1/2 cup diced onion

-1/2 cup diced celery

-1/2 cup diced carrots

-1/4 cup olive oil

-Salt and pepper to taste

-Optional herbs and spices (e.g. thyme, rosemary, garlic, etc.)

Preparation Method:

1. Preheat oven to 400°F.

2. Put the chicken breasts in a baking pan and sprinkle with salt and pepper.

3. In a separate bowl, mix together the diced onion, celery, carrots, bell peppers, olive oil, and optional herbs and spices.

4. Spread the vegetable mixture evenly over the chicken.

5. Bake in preheated oven for 20-25 minutes, or until chicken is cooked through and vegetables are tender.

6. Enjoy your meal with your favorite side dishes!

Day 26: **Breakfast**: Smoothie made with banana, 1/2 scoop of protein powder, almond milk, and 1/2 cup of oats.
Prep time: 5 minutes

Recipes:
- 1 banana
- 1/2 scoop of protein powder
- 1/2 cup almond milk
- 1/2 cup oats

Preparation Method:
1. Place the banana, protein powder, almond milk and oats in a blender.
2. Blend until smooth.
3. Enjoy!

Lunch: Hummus wrap with greens and tomatoes.
Prep Time: 10 minutes

Ingredients:
- 2 whole wheat wraps
- 2 tablespoons of hummus
- 2 cups of greens (spinach, kale, romaine, etc.)

- 1 cup of chopped tomatoes

Preparation Method:

1. Preheat a large skillet over medium heat.

2. Spread one tablespoon of hummus on each wrap.

3. Place the wraps in the skillet and cook for 1-2 minutes. Flip the wraps over and cook for an additional 1-2 minutes, or until lightly browned.

4. Remove the wraps from the skillet and place them on a plate.

5. Divide the greens and tomatoes between the two wraps.

6. Wrap the wraps up and enjoy!

Snack: A handful of almonds.

Dinner: Veggie stir-fry with brown rice.

Prep time: 15 minutes

Ingredients:

1 cup cooked brown rice

1 tablespoon olive oil

1 small onion, diced

1 red bell pepper, diced

1 small zucchini, diced

1 cup sliced mushrooms

1 teaspoon minced garlic

1 teaspoon ground ginger

2 tablespoons soy sauce

Salt and pepper, to taste

Preparation Method:

1. Put the olive oil into a big skillet and heat it over a medium-high flame.

2. Add the onion, bell pepper, zucchini, mushrooms, garlic, and ginger to the skillet and cook, stirring occasionally, until the vegetables are tender, about 5 minutes.

3. Add the cooked brown rice and soy sauce to the pan and stir to combine. Cook for an additional 2-3 minutes, until everything is heated through.

4. Season with salt and pepper to taste. Serve hot.

Day 27: **Breakfast**: Overnight oats with almond milk, banana, and chia seeds.

Prep Time: 5 minutes

Ingredients:

-1/2 cup rolled oats

-1 cup almond milk

-1 ripe banana, mashed

-2 tablespoons chia seeds

-Optional: sweetener of choice, cinnamon, nutmeg

Preparation:

1. In a medium-sized bowl, combine the rolled oats and almond milk.

2. Add the mashed banana, chia seeds, and any optional ingredients. Stir until everything is evenly combined.

3. Place the bowl in the refrigerator, and cover it with plastic wrap for storage overnight.

4. In the morning, remove the bowl from the refrigerator and serve. Enjoy!

Lunch: Turkey and vegetable wrap.

Prep Time: 10 minutes

Ingredients:

- 2 large tortillas

- 2 tablespoons mayonnaise

- 4 slices of deli-style turkey
- 1 sliced tomato
- 1/4 cup shredded lettuce
- 1/4 cup shredded cheese
- 1/4 cup diced bell pepper

Preparation Method:

1. Spread mayonnaise onto one side of each tortilla.

2. Lay the turkey, tomato, lettuce, cheese, and bell pepper onto one side of each tortilla.

3. Fold one side of the tortilla over the ingredients and then roll up the wrap to form a burrito-style wrap.

4. Slice the wrap in half and serve.

Snack: Apple slices with peanut butter.

Dinner: Baked sweet potatoes with black beans and a side salad.

Prep time: 15 minutes

Recipes:

-2 medium sweet potatoes

-1 can of black beans

-1/2 cup of chopped onions

-1/4 cup of olive oil

-1/4 cup of lime juice

-1 teaspoon of cumin

-1/2 teaspoon of chili powder

-1/2 teaspoon of garlic powder

-Salt and pepper to taste

-For the salad:

-1 head of romaine lettuce, chopped

-1/2 cup of cherry tomatoes, halved

-1/4 cup of sliced red onion

-1/4 cup of crumbled feta cheese

-2 tablespoons of olive oil

-2 tablespoons of balsamic vinegar

-Salt and pepper to taste

Preparation Method:

1. Preheat oven to 400 degrees F.

2. Prick the sweet potatoes a few times with a fork and wrap each one in aluminum foil. Place them in the oven and bake for 45-60 minutes, or until they are tender.

3. While the potatoes are baking, heat the olive oil in a large skillet over medium heat. Add the onions and cook for 5 minutes, or until softened.

4. Add the black beans, cumin, chili powder, garlic powder, salt, and pepper to the skillet. Cook for 5 minutes, stirring occasionally.

5. Once the potatoes are cooked, let them cool and then cut them into cubes. Add them to the black bean mixture and stir to combine.

6. In a separate bowl, whisk together the lime juice, olive oil, salt, and pepper.

7. To assemble the salad, combine the lettuce, tomatoes, red onion, and feta cheese in a large bowl. Drizzle with the lime juice mixture and toss to combine.

8. Serve the sweet potatoes and black beans with the side salad. Enjoy!

Day 28: **Breakfast**: Scrambled eggs with spinach and mushrooms.
Prep time: 10 minutes

Ingredients:
-3 eggs

-1/4 cup of chopped spinach

-1/4 cup of chopped mushrooms

-1 tablespoon of butter

-Salt and pepper, to taste

Preparation Method:

1.Turn the stove to medium, and place a medium non-stick skillet on the burner.

2. Add butter and let it melt.

3. Add mushrooms and spinach and sauté for 2 minutes.

4. Add eggs and season with salt and pepper.

5. Stir the eggs with a wooden spoon until they are cooked.

6. Serve hot.

Lunch: Grilled salmon with quinoa and a side salad.

Prep Time: 20 minutes

Recipes:

Grilled Salmon:

- 4 (6-ounce) salmon fillets

- 2 tablespoons olive oil

- 1 teaspoon garlic powder

- 1 teaspoon sea salt

- 1/2 teaspoon freshly ground black pepper

Quinoa:

- 1 cup quinoa

- 2 cups vegetable broth

- 1 teaspoon olive oil

- 1/4 teaspoon sea salt

Side Salad:

- 2 cups mixed greens

- 1/4 cup cherry tomatoes, halved

- 1/4 cup cucumber, diced

- 1/4 cup red onion, diced

- 2 tablespoons olive oil

- 1 tablespoon red wine vinegar

- 1/4 teaspoon sea salt

Preparation Method:

1. Preheat the grill to medium-high heat.

2. Rub the salmon fillets with the olive oil, garlic powder, sea salt, and pepper. Place the fillets on

the preheated grill and cook for 4-5 minutes per side, or until the salmon is cooked through.

3. Meanwhile, prepare the quinoa. In a medium saucepan, combine the quinoa, vegetable broth, olive oil, and sea salt. Bring the mixture to a boil, reduce the heat to low, and simmer for 15 minutes, or until the quinoa is cooked through.

4. To make the side salad, combine the mixed greens, cherry tomatoes, cucumber, and red onion in a bowl. In a separate bowl, whisk together the olive oil, red wine vinegar, and sea salt. Pour the dressing onto the salad and mix it together.

5. Serve the grilled salmon with the quinoa and side salad. Enjoy!

Snack: Greek yogurt with berries.
Dinner: Baked fish with roasted broccoli.
Prep Time: 15 minutes

Ingredients:
- 2 fillets of white fish (such as cod, haddock, or pollock)
- 2 cups of broccoli florets
- 2 tablespoons of olive oil

- 1/2 teaspoon of garlic powder

- Salt and pepper, to taste

Preparation Method:

1. Preheat the oven to 400 degrees Fahrenheit.

2. Cover a baking sheet with parchment paper.

3. Put the fish fillets onto the baking sheet.

4. Mix together the broccoli florets, olive oil, garlic powder, salt, and pepper in a bowl.

5. Place the broccoli on the baking sheet around the fish.

6. Bake for 15 minutes.

7. Serve warm. Enjoy!

Day 29: **Breakfast**: Yogurt bowl with fruit and nuts.
Prep Time: 10 minutes

Ingredients:

- 1 cup plain yogurt

- 1/2 cup fresh fruit (such as blueberries, strawberries, or peaches)

- 1/4 cup chopped nuts or seeds (such as almonds, walnuts, or sunflower seeds)

- Honey or maple syrup (optional)

- Shredded coconut (optional)

- Granola (optional)

Preparation method:

1. Place the yogurt in a bowl.

2. Top with the fresh fruit, nuts or seeds.

3. Drizzle with honey or maple syrup and sprinkle with shredded coconut and granola, if desired.

4. Serve and enjoy!

Lunch: Chicken soup with quinoa.

Prep Time : 10 minutes

Recipe:

- 2 cups of chicken broth

- 1 cup of quinoa

- 1 cup of diced carrots

- 1 cup of diced celery

- 1/2 cup of diced onion

- 2 cloves of garlic, minced

- 1 teaspoon of dried thyme

- 2 tablespoons of olive oil

- Salt and pepper to taste

Preparation Method:

1. In a large pot, set the heat to medium-high and add the olive oil to begin heating.

2. Add the onions, celery, carrots and garlic and cook until they are softened, about 5 minutes.

3. Add the chicken broth, quinoa and thyme. Bring to a boil, then reduce the heat to low and simmer for 10 minutes.

4. Season with salt and pepper to taste.

5. Serve the soup hot. Enjoy!

Snack: A handful of nuts.

Dinner: Roasted vegetables with quinoa.

Prep Time: 10 minutes

Ingredients:

- 2 cups of cooked quinoa

- 2 cups of mixed vegetables (such as broccoli, cauliflower, bell peppers, mushrooms, etc.)

- 1 tablespoon olive oil

- 1 teaspoon garlic powder

- 1 teaspoon Italian seasoning

- Salt and pepper to taste

Preparation Method:

1. Preheat oven to 400°F (200°C).

2. Place the vegetables in a large bowl and drizzle with olive oil. Sprinkle garlic powder, Italian seasoning, salt, and pepper over the vegetables.

3. Toss the vegetables until they are evenly coated with the oil and seasonings.

4. Layer the vegetables on a baking sheet in an even distribution.

5. Roast for 25 minutes or until the vegetables are tender and lightly browned.

6. Meanwhile, prepare the quinoa according to package instructions.

7. Place the cooked quinoa in a large bowl and add the roasted vegetables. Stir to combine.

8. Serve warm. Enjoy!

Day 30: **Breakfast**: Avocado toast with poached eggs.

Prep Time: 10 minutes

Ingredients:
- 2 slices of bread

- 1 avocado

- 2 eggs

- 1 tablespoon of white vinegar

- Salt and pepper to taste

- Optional: red pepper flakes and/or chives

Preparation Method:

1. Bring a pot of water to a boil, then reduce heat to a simmer.

2. Toast the bread slices until they are golden brown.

3. Begin by cutting the avocado in half, then take out the pit. Scoop out the flesh and place it in a bowl. Use a fork to mash the avocado until it is creamy. Spread the mashed avocado onto each slice of toasted bread.

4. Crack the eggs into the simmering water, one at a time. Add the vinegar to help keep the whites together. Cook for 3-4 minutes, or until the whites are cooked through but yolks are still soft.

5. Remove the eggs using a slotted spoon, and place one egg on top of each slice of avocado toast. Sprinkle with salt and pepper, and any other desired toppings. Enjoy!

Lunch: Tuna salad with avocado and cucumber.

Prep Time: 10 minutes

Ingredients:

-2 cans tuna in water, drained

-1/2 diced avocado

-1 diced cucumber

-1/4 cup diced onion

-1/4 cup diced celery

-1/4 cup mayonnaise

-2 tablespoons lemon juice

-Salt and pepper, to taste

Preparation Method:

1. In a bowl, combine the tuna, avocado, cucumber, onion, and celery.

2. In a separate bowl, whisk together the mayonnaise, lemon juice, salt, and pepper.

3. Pour the mayonnaise mixture over the tuna mixture and stir until everything is evenly coated.

4. Serve the tuna salad with extra diced avocado, cucumber, and onion as desired.

Enjoy!

Snack: Celery sticks with hummus.

Dinner: Baked tofu with roasted veggies.

Prep Time: 30 minutes

Ingredients:

-1 block of extra firm tofu

-1 bell pepper, cut into slices

-1/2 red onion, sliced

-1/2 head of broccoli, cut into florets

-1 zucchini, sliced

-1/4 cup of olive oil

-2 cloves of garlic, minced

-2 tablespoons of soy sauce

-1 tablespoon of maple syrup

-Salt and pepper to taste

Preparation Method:

1. Preheat oven to 400°F.

2. Drain and press tofu for 10 minutes. Cube the food and put it in a bowl.

3. Add bell pepper, onion, broccoli and zucchini to the bowl with the tofu.

4. In a small bowl, mix together olive oil, garlic, soy sauce and maple syrup. Pour over the tofu and veggies and toss to coat.

5. Spread the tofu and veggies on a baking sheet and season with salt and pepper.

6. Bake for 20-25 minutes, stirring once halfway through, until vegetables are tender and tofu is golden and crispy.

7. Serve warm. Enjoy!

Chapter 8: Exercise and Intermittent Fasting

Exercise with intermittent fasting can be a powerful health-promoting combination for women over 60. Intermittent fasting is a way of eating that involves alternating between periods of eating and periods of abstaining from food. It can help to improve overall health and wellbeing by providing a range of physical and mental benefits. Combined with exercise, intermittent fasting can provide a range of additional benefits specifically for women over 60, including:

Weight Loss: Intermittent fasting combined with regular exercise can help to promote healthy weight loss. Studies have shown that women over 60 who practice intermittent fasting and exercise have a higher success rate for achieving and maintaining healthy body weight.

Improved Metabolism: Intermittent fasting combined with exercise can help to improve metabolic health by increasing energy expenditure and boosting metabolism. This can help to reduce the risk of chronic health conditions such as diabetes and heart disease.

Reduced Inflammation: Intermittent fasting combined with exercise can help to reduce inflammation in the body. This can minimize the chances of developing chronic conditions and enhance overall well-being.

Improved Cognitive Function: Intermittent fasting combined with exercise can help to improve cognitive function in women over 60. Studies have shown that regular physical activity can help to reduce age-related cognitive decline and improve memory and concentration.

Improved Heart Health: Intermittent fasting combined with exercise can also help to improve heart health by reducing bad cholesterol and increasing good cholesterol. This may lessen the likelihood of suffering from a cardiac arrest, cerebrovascular accident, and other cardiovascular illnesses.

Improved Mental Health: Intermittent fasting combined with exercise can also help to improve mental health in women over 60. Regular physical activity can help to reduce stress and anxiety, improve mood, and promote a positive outlook.

Intermittent fasting combined with exercise can help to improve overall health and wellbeing in women over 60. It can help to promote healthy weight loss, improve metabolic health, reduce inflammation, and improve cognitive and heart health. It can also help to improve mental health by reducing stress and anxiety and promoting a positive outlook.

Therefore it is recommended that women over 60 should consider incorporating intermittent fasting into their lifestyle, along with regular physical activity, to achieve optimal health and wellbeing.

60 days exercise plan for women over 60

Day 1:
- Wake up and do 5 minutes of gentle stretching.
- Practice intermittent fasting for 16 hours and eat within 8 hours.
- Start light exercises such as jogging in place or walking for 15 minutes.

Day 2:
- Wake up and do 5 minutes of gentle stretching.
- Practice intermittent fasting for 16 hours and eat within 8 hours.
- Spend 30 minutes doing light cardio exercises such as walking or jogging.

Day 3:
- Wake up and do 5 minutes of gentle stretching.
- Practice intermittent fasting for 16 hours and eat within 8 hours.
- Spend 30 minutes doing strength training exercises such as squats and lunges.

Day 4:

- Wake up and do 5 minutes of gentle stretching.

- Practice intermittent fasting for 16 hours and eat within 8 hours.

- Spend 30 minutes doing yoga or Pilates.

Day 5:

- Wake up and do 5 minutes of gentle stretching.

- Practice intermittent fasting for 16 hours and eat within 8 hours.

- Spend 30 minutes doing light cardio exercises such as walking or jogging.

Day 6:

- Wake up and do 5 minutes of gentle stretching.

- Practice intermittent fasting for 16 hours and eat within 8 hours.

- Spend 30 minutes doing strength training exercises such as squats and lunges.

Day 7:

- Rest day.

- Practice intermittent fasting for 16 hours and eat within 8 hours.

Day 8:

- Wake up and do 5 minutes of gentle stretching.

- Practice intermittent fasting for 16 hours and eat within 8 hours.

- Spend 30 minutes doing light cardio exercises such as walking or jogging.

Day 9:

- Wake up and do 5 minutes of gentle stretching.

- Practice intermittent fasting for 16 hours and eat within 8 hours.

- Spend 30 minutes doing strength training exercises such as squats and lunges.

Day 10:

- Wake up and do 5 minutes of gentle stretching.

- Practice intermittent fasting for 16 hours and eat within 8 hours.

- Spend 30 minutes doing yoga or Pilates.

Day 11:

- Wake up and do 5 minutes of gentle stretching.

- Practice intermittent fasting for 16 hours and eat within 8 hours.
- Spend 30 minutes doing light cardio exercises such as walking or jogging.

Day 12:
- Wake up and do 5 minutes of gentle stretching.
- Practice intermittent fasting for 16 hours and eat within 8 hours.
- Spend 30 minutes doing strength training exercises such as squats and lunges.

Day 13:
- Rest day.
- Practice intermittent fasting for 16 hours and eat within 8 hours.

Day 14:
- Wake up and do 5 minutes of gentle stretching.
- Practice intermittent fasting for 16 hours and eat within 8 hours.
- Spend 30 minutes doing light cardio exercises such as walking or jogging.

Day 15:

- Wake up and do 5 minutes of gentle stretching.

- Practice intermittent fasting for 16 hours and eat within 8 hours.

- Spend 30 minutes doing strength training exercises such as squats and lunges.

Day 16:

- Wake up and do 5 minutes of gentle stretching.

- Practice intermittent fasting for 16 hours and eat within 8 hours.

- Spend 30 minutes doing yoga or Pilates.

Day 17:

- Wake up and do 5 minutes of gentle stretching.

- Practice intermittent fasting for 16 hours and eat within 8 hours.

- Spend 30 minutes doing light cardio exercises such as walking or jogging.

Day 18:

- Wake up and do 5 minutes of gentle stretching.

- Practice intermittent fasting for 16 hours and eat within 8 hours.

- Spend 30 minutes doing strength training exercises such as squats and lunges.

Day 19:
- Rest day.
- Practice intermittent fasting for 16 hours and eat within 8 hours.

Day 20:
- Wake up and do 5 minutes of gentle stretching.
- Practice intermittent fasting for 16 hours and eat within 8 hours.
- Spend 30 minutes doing light cardio exercises such as walking or jogging.

Day 21:
- Wake up and do 5 minutes of gentle stretching.
- Practice intermittent fasting for 16 hours and eat within 8 hours.
- Spend 30 minutes doing strength training exercises such as squats and lunges.

Day 22:
- Wake up and do 5 minutes of gentle stretching.

- Practice intermittent fasting for 16 hours and eat within 8 hours.
- Spend 30 minutes doing yoga or Pilates.

Day 23:
- Wake up and do 5 minutes of gentle stretching.
- Practice intermittent fasting for 16 hours and eat within 8 hours.
- Spend 30 minutes doing light cardio exercises such as walking or jogging.

Day 24:
- Wake up and do 5 minutes of gentle stretching.
- Practice intermittent fasting for 16 hours and eat within 8 hours.
- Spend 30 minutes doing strength training exercises such as squats and lunges.

Day 25:
- Rest day.
- Practice intermittent fasting for 16 hours and eat within 8 hours.

Day 26:

- Wake up and do 5 minutes of gentle stretching.
- Practice intermittent fasting for 16 hours and eat within 8 hours.
- Spend 30 minutes doing light cardio exercises such as walking or jogging.

Day 27:
- Wake up and do 5 minutes of gentle stretching.
- Practice intermittent fasting for 16 hours and eat within 8 hours.
- Spend 30 minutes doing strength training exercises such as squats and lunges.

Day 28:
- Wake up and do 5 minutes of gentle stretching.
- Practice intermittent fasting for 16 hours and eat within 8 hours.
- Spend 30 minutes doing yoga or Pilates.

Day 29:
- Wake up and do 5 minutes of gentle stretching.
- Practice intermittent fasting for 16 hours and eat within 8 hours.

- Spend 30 minutes doing light cardio exercises such as walking or jogging.

Day 30:
- Wake up and do 5 minutes of gentle stretching.
- Practice intermittent fasting for 16 hours and eat within 8 hours.
- Spend 30 minutes doing strength training exercises such as squats and lunges.

Day 31:
- Rest day.
- Practice intermittent fasting for 16 hours and eat within 8 hours.

Day 32:
- Wake up and do 5 minutes of gentle stretching.
- Practice intermittent fasting for 16 hours and eat within 8 hours.
- Spend 30 minutes doing light cardio exercises such as walking or jogging.

Day 33:
- Wake up and do 5 minutes of gentle stretching.

- Practice intermittent fasting for 16 hours and eat within 8 hours.
- Spend 30 minutes doing strength training exercises such as squats and lunges.

Day 34:
- Wake up and do 5 minutes of gentle stretching.
- Practice intermittent fasting for 16 hours and eat within 8 hours.
- Spend 30 minutes doing yoga or Pilates.

Day 35:
- Wake up and do 5 minutes of gentle stretching.
- Practice intermittent fasting for 16 hours and eat within 8 hours.
- Spend 30 minutes doing light cardio exercises such as walking or jogging.

Day 36:
- Wake up and do 5 minutes of gentle stretching.
- Practice intermittent fasting for 16 hours and eat within 8 hours.
- Spend 30 minutes doing strength training exercises such as squats and lunges.

Day 37:

- Rest day.

- Practice intermittent fasting for 16 hours and eat within 8 hours.

Day 38:

- Wake up and do 5 minutes of gentle stretching.

- Practice intermittent fasting for 16 hours and eat within 8 hours.

- Spend 30 minutes doing light cardio exercises such as walking or jogging.

Day 39:

- Wake up and do 5 minutes of gentle stretching.

- Practice intermittent fasting for 16 hours and eat within 8 hours.

- Spend 30 minutes doing strength training exercises such as squats and lunges.

Day 40:

- Wake up and do 5 minutes of gentle stretching.

- Practice intermittent fasting for 16 hours and eat within 8 hours.
- Spend 30 minutes doing yoga or Pilates.

Day 41:
- Wake up and do 5 minutes of gentle stretching.
- Practice intermittent fasting for 16 hours and eat within 8 hours.
- Spend 30 minutes doing light cardio exercises such as walking or jogging.

Day 42:
- Wake up and do 5 minutes of gentle stretching.
- Practice intermittent fasting for 16 hours and eat within 8 hours.
- Spend 30 minutes doing strength training exercises such as squats and lunges.

Day 43:
- Rest day.
- Practice intermittent fasting for 16 hours and eat within 8 hours.

Day 44:

- Wake up and do 5 minutes of gentle stretching.
- Practice intermittent fasting for 16 hours and eat within 8 hours.
- Spend 30 minutes doing light cardio exercises such as walking or jogging.

Day 45:
- Wake up and do 5 minutes of gentle stretching.
- Practice intermittent fasting for 16 hours and eat within 8 hours.
- Spend 30 minutes doing strength training exercises such as squats and lunges.

Day 46:
- Wake up and do 5 minutes of gentle stretching.
- Practice intermittent fasting for 16 hours and eat within 8 hours.
- Spend 30 minutes doing yoga or Pilates.

Day 47:
- Wake up and do 5 minutes of gentle stretching.
- Practice intermittent fasting for 16 hours and eat within 8 hours.

- Spend 30 minutes doing light cardio exercises such as walking or jogging.

Day 48:
- Wake up and do 5 minutes of gentle stretching.
- Practice intermittent fasting for 16 hours and eat within 8 hours.
- Spend 30 minutes doing strength training exercises such as squats and lunges.

Day 49:
- Rest day.
- Practice intermittent fasting for 16 hours and eat within 8 hours.

Day 50:
- Wake up and do 5 minutes of gentle stretching.
- Practice intermittent fasting for 16 hours and eat within 8 hours.
- Spend 30 minutes doing light cardio exercises such as walking or jogging.

Day 51:
- Wake up and do 5 minutes of gentle stretching.

- Practice intermittent fasting for 16 hours and eat within 8 hours.
- Spend 30 minutes doing strength training exercises such as squats and lunges.

Day 52:
- Wake up and do 5 minutes of gentle stretching.
- Practice intermittent fasting for 16 hours and eat within 8 hours.
- Spend 30 minutes doing yoga or Pilates.

Day 53:
- Wake up and do 5 minutes of gentle stretching.
- Practice intermittent fasting for 16 hours and eat within 8 hours.
- Spend 30 minutes doing light cardio exercises such as walking or jogging.

Day 54:
- Wake up and do 5 minutes of gentle stretching.
- Practice intermittent fasting for 16 hours and eat within 8 hours.
- Spend 30 minutes doing strength training exercises such as squats and lunges.

Day 55:

- Rest day.

- Practice intermittent fasting for 16 hours and eat within 8 hours.

Day 56:

- Wake up and do 5 minutes of gentle stretching.

- Practice intermittent fasting for 16 hours and eat within 8 hours.

- Spend 30 minutes doing light cardio exercises such as walking or jogging.

Day 57:

- Wake up and do 5 minutes of gentle stretching.

- Practice intermittent fasting for 16 hours and eat within 8 hours.

- Spend 30 minutes doing strength training exercises such as squats and lunges.

Day 58:

- Wake up and do 5 minutes of gentle stretching.

- Practice intermittent fasting for 16 hours and eat within 8 hours.

- Spend 30 minutes doing yoga or Pilates.

Day 59:
- Wake up and do 5 minutes of gentle stretching.
- Practice intermittent fasting for 16 hours and eat within 8 hours.
- Spend 30 minutes doing light cardio exercises such as walking or jogging.

Day 60:
- Wake up and do 5 minutes of gentle stretching.
- Practice intermittent fasting for 16 hours and eat within 8 hours.
- Spend 30 minutes doing strength training exercises such as squats and lunges.
- Spend the remaining time relaxing and enjoying your newfound energy from your plan.

Part Three:

Troubleshooting and Tips

Troubleshooting:

1. Make sure you are taking in enough nutrients. Intermittent fasting involves limited intake of food and nutrients, so it is important that the meals you do eat are packed with nutrition. Make sure you are including plenty of fruits, vegetables, lean proteins, and healthy fats.

2. Monitor your energy levels. Intermittent fasting can cause fatigue, so it is important to keep an eye on your energy levels. If you find yourself feeling sluggish, make sure you are still getting enough rest and are drinking enough water.

3. Check for signs of dehydration. Dehydration is a common side effect of intermittent fasting, so make sure you are staying hydrated by drinking at least 8 glasses of water per day. If you are still feeling

dehydrated, consider adding electrolyte-rich drinks to your diet.

4. Pay attention to hunger cues. When intermittent fasting, it is important to listen to your body and eat when you are actually hungry. If you find yourself feeling hungry but are not ready for a meal, try drinking a glass of water or snacking on a piece of fruit.

Tips for Intermittent Fasting for Women Over 60:

1. Start slowly. Intermittent fasting may be intimidating for women over 60, so it is important to start slowly. Try fasting for 12 hours or less before gradually increasing the amount of time you fast.

2. Stick to a schedule. Sticking to a regular schedule will help make intermittent fasting easier. Choose a time to start fasting each day, and make sure you are eating all your meals within a set time frame.

3. Choose nutrient-dense foods. Intermittent fasting requires limiting your intake of food and nutrients, so it is important to make sure the meals you do eat are packed with nutrition. Choose foods that are high in protein, fiber, healthy fats, and vitamins and minerals.

4. Drink plenty of fluids. Drinking plenty of fluids, particularly water, throughout the day is essential for staying hydrated during intermittent fasting. Make sure to drink at least 8 glasses of water per day to help prevent dehydration.

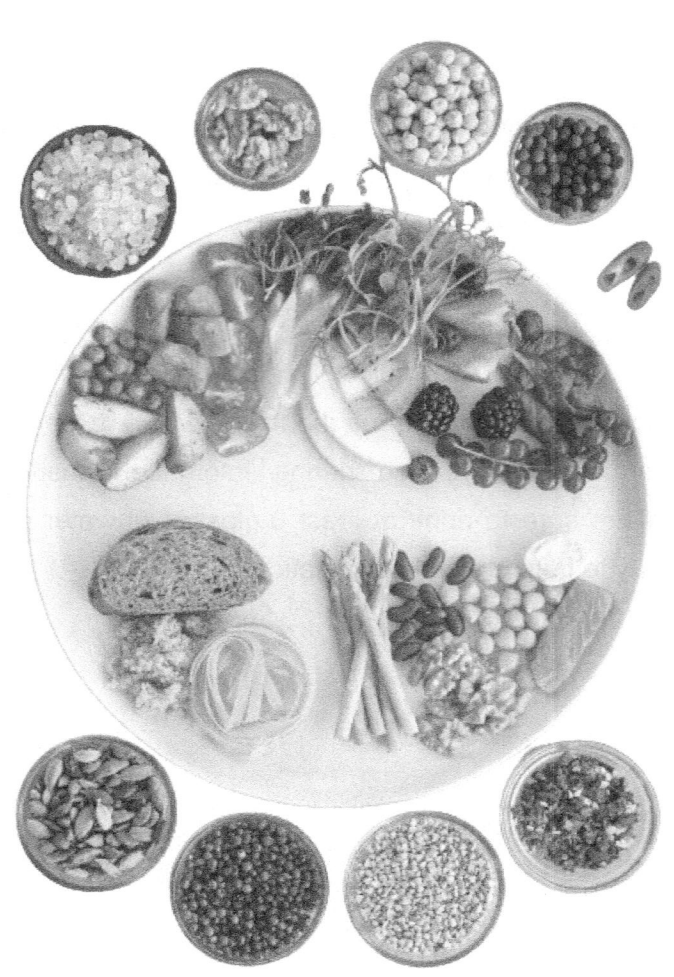

Chapter 9: Common Challenges with Intermittent Fasting

Intermittent fasting is a popular diet trend that involves reducing or eliminating food consumption for a period of time and then resuming regular eating habits. While this type of dieting has become popular due to its potential health benefits, it can also come with some common challenges.

One of the most common challenges with intermittent fasting is dealing with hunger. Since the body is used to eating regularly, it can take some time to adjust to going without food. This can lead to feelings of hunger, cravings, and irritability during fasting periods. It can also be difficult to stick to the fasting plan if these feelings become too overwhelming.

A challenge is dealing with social situations. When following an intermittent fasting plan, social activities that involve eating, such as going out to dinner or having lunch with friends, can be difficult to manage. It's important to be prepared with snacks and drinks to avoid temptation or feeling left out.

Intermittent fasting can also be hard on the body if it's not done properly. It's important to make sure you are getting enough nutrients from the food you do eat, and to make sure that you are taking breaks from fasting when needed.

Another common challenge with intermittent fasting is dealing with cravings. Many people find it difficult to ignore their cravings, especially if they have a sweet tooth. It is important to find healthy ways to satisfy cravings during fasting periods, such as drinking unsweetened tea or coffee and eating high-fiber snacks.

It can be difficult to stick to a regular intermittent fasting schedule. Life can get in the way of maintaining a consistent fasting schedule, such as travel, illness, or simply forgetting to fast. It is important to plan ahead and be prepared for days when fasting is not possible. This will help ensure that you can stay on track with your fasting program.

Finally, it can be difficult to maintain an intermittent fasting plan for the long term. This type of diet is not for everyone, and it's important to make sure it's the right choice for you before committing to it.

Chapter 10: Tips for Success with Intermittent Fasting

Intermittent fasting is a popular dieting strategy that has been gaining traction in recent years. It involves alternating periods of eating with periods of fasting, usually lasting anywhere from 12 to 24 hours. There are many different ways to do intermittent fasting, and it can be a great way to jumpstart your weight loss journey. Here are some tips to help you make the most out of your intermittent fasting experience.

1. Start slow: It's important to ease into intermittent fasting, especially if you're new to it. Start with shorter fasts of 12-14 hours and gradually work your way up to longer fasts. This will give your body time to adjust and get used to the new routine.

2. Choose the right fasting window: Choose a fasting window that works for your lifestyle and schedule. Some popular fasting windows are the 16/8 method (fasting for 16 hours and eating all of your meals within an 8-hour window) or the 5:2 diet

(eating normally for 5 days and fasting for two days).

3. Eat nutrient-dense foods: Intermittent fasting doesn't mean you can eat whatever you want. You should still focus on eating nutritious foods and avoiding processed and unhealthy foods. Eating nutrient-dense foods will help you stay satiated and energized during your fasting periods.

4. Stay hydrated: It's important to stay hydrated when intermittent fasting. Aim to drink at least 8 glasses of water a day, and drink more if you're exercising or sweating heavily. You can also drink unsweetened tea and coffee to help curb hunger during fasting periods.

5. Get enough sleep: Sleep is essential for weight loss and overall health. Aim for 7-8 hours of sleep each night to ensure you're well-rested and energized for the day.

6. Be mindful of your portions: Be mindful of your portion sizes when eating. Eating too much during

your eating periods can negate the benefits of intermittent fasting.

7. Track your progress: Tracking your progress is key to success with intermittent fasting. Use an app or website to log your meals and track your weight loss. This will help you stay motivated and on track with your goals.

Intermittent fasting can be a powerful tool for weight loss, but it's important to do it correctly. Follow these tips to get the most out of your intermittent fasting experience.

Conclusion

Intermittent fasting has been a popular topic among women over 60 in recent years. Many women choose to adopt this lifestyle to improve their health, lose weight, and even reduce the risk of certain diseases. While the benefits of intermittent fasting are promising, it is important to understand the potential risks that come along with it, particularly for women over 60.

Intermittent fasting involves intentionally skipping meals and restricting caloric intake for a period of time. This can be done in various ways, such as 16:8 fasting (16 hours of fasting and 8 hours of eating) or 5:2 fasting (5 days of normal eating and 2 days of severe calorie restriction). While intermittent fasting can be beneficial for many women over 60, it is important to consider the potential risks before making any major changes to your diet.

Women over 60 may be particularly vulnerable to the side effects of intermittent fasting. As the body ages, it becomes less efficient at utilizing stored energy, so it is important to maintain a balanced nutritional intake to ensure adequate energy and nutrients. Additionally, women over 60 may be more prone to dehydration due to decreased thirst sensation, and fasting can further increase this risk. Finally, fasting can also lead to nutrient deficiencies, particularly in vitamins and minerals like iron, vitamin B12, and folate.

To minimize the risks associated with intermittent fasting, it is important to be mindful of your nutrition. Make sure to consult with a healthcare professional before making any major changes to your diet, and make sure to get adequate nutrition from a balanced diet even when fasting. Additionally, it is important to stay hydrated and supplement your diet with vitamins and minerals as needed.

In conclusion, intermittent fasting can be a beneficial lifestyle for many women over 60. However, it is important to consider the potential risks and make sure to maintain adequate nutrition, hydration, and vitamin and mineral intake. With the proper precaution and preparation, intermittent fasting can be a safe and healthy way to improve overall health and wellbeing.

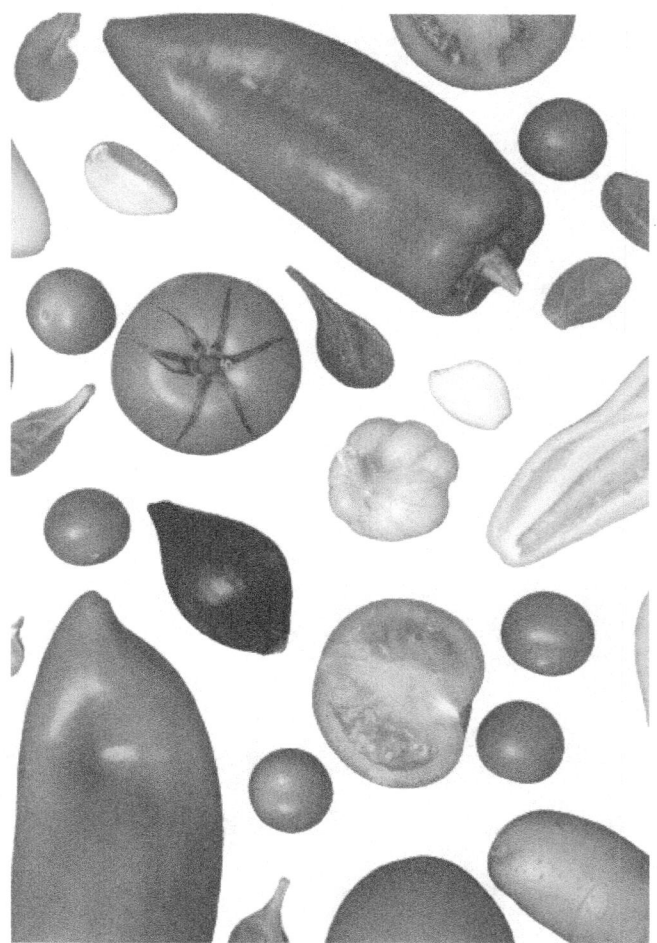

Intermittent Fasting Timetable

Days	Activity	Remarks
1		
2		
3		
4		

5		
6		
7		
8		
9		
10		

11		
12		
13		
14		
15		
16		

17		
18		
19		

20		
21		
22		

23		
24		
25		
26		
27		
28		

29		

30		

Made in the USA
Coppell, TX
23 September 2023

21926709R00109